CYBERSAFETY

Cyberstalking and Cyberbullying

CYBERSAFETY

CYBERSAFETY

Cyberstalking and Cyberbullying

SAMUEL C. MCQUADE, III, PH.D.,
SARAH E. GENTRY, AND NATHAN W. FISK

MARCUS K. ROGERS, PH.D.,
CONSULTING EDITOR

CHELSEA HOUSE
An Infobase Learning Company

Cybersafety: Cyberstalking and Cyberbullying

Chelsea House
An Infobase Learning Company
132 West 31st Street
New York, NY 10001

Library of Congress Cataloging-in-Publication Data

McQuade, Samuel C.
  Cyberstalking and Cyberbullying / Samuel C. McQuade, Sarah Gentry and Nathan Fisk ; Marcus K. Rogers, consulting editor.
     p. cm. — (Cybersafety)
  Includes bibliographical references and index.
  ISBN-13: 978-1-60413-695-1 (hardcover : alk. paper)
  ISBN-10: 1-60413-695-2 (hardcover : alk. paper) 1. Cyberbullying. 2. Cyberstalking. I. Gentry, Sarah. II. Fisk, Nathan W. III. Rogers, Marcus K. IV. Title. V. Series.

  HV6773.15.C92M37 2011
  302.3—dc22

                                   2011005641

Text design by Erik Lindstrom
Composition by Kerry Casey
Cover design by Takeshi Takahashi
Cover printed by Yurchak Printing, Landisville, Pa.
Book printed and bound by Yurchak Printing, Landisville, Pa.
Date printed: March 2012

Printed in the United States of America

This book is printed on acid-free paper.

CONTENTS

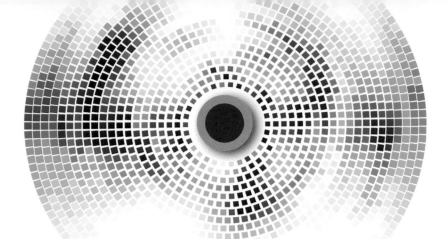

Foreword

The Internet has had and will continue to have a profound effect on society. It is hard to imagine life without such technologies as computers, cell phones, gaming devices, and so on. The Internet, World Wide Web, and their associated technologies have altered our social and personal experience of the world. In no other time in history have we had such access to knowledge and raw information. One can search the Library of Congress, the Louvre in Paris, and read online books and articles or watch videos from just about any country in the world. We can interact and chat with friends down the street, in another state, or halfway around the globe. The world is now our neighborhood. We are a "wired" society that lives a significant amount of our life online and tethered to technology.

The Internet, or cyberspace, is a great enabler. What is also becoming apparent, though, is that there is a dark side to this global wired society. As the concept of who our friends are moves from real world relationships to cyberspace connections, so also do the rules change regarding social conventions and norms. How many friends do we have online that we have actually met in person? Are online-only friends even real or at the very least whom they claim to be? We also begin to redefine privacy. Questions arise over what should be considered private or public information. Do we really want everyone in the global society to have access to our personal information? As with the real world there may be people online that we do not wish to associate with or grant access to our lives.

It is easy to become enamored with technology and the technology/information revolution. It is equally as easy to become paranoid about the dangers inherent in cyberspace. What is difficult but necessary is to be realistic about how our world has been forever changed. We see numerous magazine, TV, and newspaper headlines regarding the latest cybercrime attacks. Stories about identity theft being the fastest growing nonviolent criminal activity are common. The government is concerned with cyber or information warfare attacks against critical infrastructures. Given this kind of media coverage it is easy to think that the sky is falling and cyberspace is somehow evil. Yet if we step back and think about it, technology is neither good nor bad, it simply *is*. Technology is neutral; it is what we do with technology that determines whether it improves our lives or damages and makes our lives more difficult. Even if someone is on the proverbial fence over whether the Internet and cyberspace are society enablers or disablers, what is certain is that the technology genie is out of the bottle. We will never be able to put it back in; we need to learn how to master and live with it.

Learning to live with the Internet and its technological offshoots is one of the objectives behind the Cybersafety series of books. The immortal words of Sir Francis Bacon (the father of the scientific method), "knowledge is power," ring especially true today. If we live in a society that is dependent on technology and therefore we live a significant portion of our daily lives in cyberspace, then we need to understand the potential downside as well as the upside. However, what is not useful is fear mongering or the demonization of technology.

There is no doubt that cyberspace has its share of bad actors and criminals. This should not come as a surprise to anyone. Cyberspace mirrors traditional society, including both the good and unfortunately the bad. Historically criminals have been attracted to new technologies in an effort to improve and extend their criminal methods. The same advantages that technology and cyberspace bring to our normal everyday lives (e.g., increased communication, the ability to remotely access information) can be used in a criminal manner. Online fraud, identity theft, cyberstalking, and cyberbullying are but a few of the ugly behaviors that we see online today.

Navigating successfully through cyberspace also means that we need to understand how the "cyber" affects our personality and social behavior. One of the empowering facets of cyberspace and technology is the fact that we can escape reality and find creative outlets for ourselves. We can immerse ourselves in computer and online games, and if so inclined, satisfy our desire to gamble or engage in other risky behaviors. The sense of anonymity and the ability to redefine who we are online can be intoxicating to some people. We can experiment with new roles and behaviors that may be polar opposites of who we are in the real physical world. Yet, as in the real world, our activities and behaviors in cyberspace have consequences too. Well-meaning escapism can turn to online addictions; seemingly harmless distractions like online gaming can consume so much of our time that our real world relationships and lives are negatively affected. The presumed anonymity afforded by cyberspace can lead to bullying and stalking, behaviors that can have a profound and damaging impact on the victims and on ourselves.

The philosophy behind the Cybersafety series is based on the recognition that cyberspace and technology will continue to play an increasingly important part of our everyday lives. The way in which we define who we are, our home life, school, social relationships, and work life will all be influenced and impacted by our online behaviors and misbehaviors. Our historical notions of privacy will also be redefined in terms of universal access to our everyday activities and posted musings. The Cybersafety series was created to assist us in understanding and making sense of the online world. The intended audience for the series is those individuals who are and will be the most directly affected by cyberspace and its technologies, namely young people (i.e., those in grades 6 -12).

Young people are the future of our society. It is they who will go forward and shape societal norms, customs, public policy, draft new laws, and be our leaders. They will be tasked with developing positive coping mechanisms for both the physical and cyberworlds. They will have dual citizenship responsibilities: citizens of the physical and of the cyber. It is hoped that this series will assist in providing insight, guidance, and positive advice for this journey.

The series is divided into books that logically gather related concepts and issues. The goal of each book in the series is not to scare but to educate and inform the reader. As the title of the series states the focus is on "safety." Each book in the series provides advice on what to watch out for and how to be safer. The emphasis is on education and awareness while providing a frank discussion related to the consequences of certain online behaviors.

It is my sincere pleasure and honor to be associated with this series. As a former law enforcement officer and current educator, I am all too aware of the dangers that can befall our young people. I am also keenly aware that young people are more astute than some adults commonly give them credit for being. Therefore it is imperative that we begin a dialogue that enhances our awareness and encourages and challenges the reader to reexamine their behaviors and attitudes toward cyberspace and technology. We fear what we do not understand; fear is not productive, but knowledge is empowering. So let's begin our collective journey into arming ourselves with more knowledge.

—Marcus K. Rogers, Ph.D., CISSP, DFCP,
Founder and Director,
Cyber Forensics Program,
Purdue University

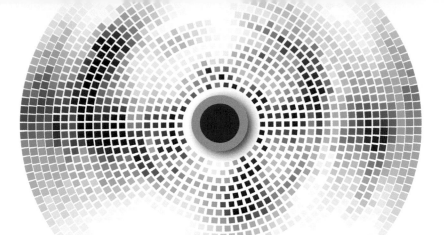

Introduction: Cyberstalking and Cyberbullying Defined

Ryan Halligan, a 13-year-old boy living in Vermont, had endured abuse from his classmates on a fairly regular basis, both in school and online. Some kids in school had constantly accused him of being gay. One time a girl pretended to be romantically interested in him only as a way to trick him into revealing personal secrets, which other students later posted online and mocked. To most of his classmates and friends, Ryan was just an ordinary kid who was bullied daily. His father did not grasp the seriousness of the bullying situation and considered taking Ryan's computer away because his school grades declined. For Ryan, however, constant online and in-person abuse became unbearable. When a new school year started, he became increasingly depressed and began to discuss suicide online. In an online chat found on Ryan's computer, one bully encouraged him to kill himself:

> *Bully: ur finally gonna kill urself?*
> *Ryan: yep*

Bully: phew – its about f***ing time

Ryan: you'll hear about it in the papers tomorrow

Ryan did not immediately follow through on his threat. However, on October 7, 2003, two weeks after the chat, he was found dead, having hanged himself in a bathroom at home.[1]

What happened to Ryan Halligan illustrates a tragic ending to a life interrupted needlessly by cyberbullying. The people who bullied Ryan along with fellow students who stood idly by as he was bullied, or who knew or should have known more about what Ryan was experiencing, are all at least partially responsible for his death. An entire school and community were negatively affected, with many individuals scarred forever by Ryan's untimely death.

Prior to widespread use of the Internet, young people who bullied did so in their neighborhoods and on school grounds. Similarly, traditional, off-line stalking occurred when a stalker followed someone around from one place to another. Bullying has evolved over generations and bullies have used various tools and methods in harming their victims. An anonymous threat sent through conventional ("snail") mail is another way to bully. A person who writes an antigay slur on someone's locker using a permanent marker is also bullying and perhaps remaining anonymous in the process, which creates fear about who wrote the message. Likewise, a person who shouts a racist slur to belittle someone in front of a crowd of peers causes anger and fear even if the bully is not anonymous. Whether a bully uses a marker or shouts, the hateful message(s) is broadcast to everyone who reads the slur, hears the shout, or later hears about what happened from friends.

Bullies harm their victims by communicating their message either directly or indirectly. Technological devices can assist them in doing so. During the 1800s, telegraph and telephone systems allowed bullies to communicate insulting, harassing, and threatening messages. Telegraph and phone operators had the ability to listen into conversations and gossip about private, personal information sent "over the wires." Before phones were programmed with caller ID, bullies could make multiple phone calls to their victim,

In 2003, John Halligan's son, Ryan, committed suicide after being bullied online. *(Source: AP Photo/Toby Talbot)*

scream or whistle into microphones, or simply hang up once their call was answered and remain anonymous. As a result, bullies were able to use earlier forms of communication technologies to harass, intimidate, threaten, gossip, or coerce their victims into doing things they would not otherwise have done.

WHAT IS CYBERBULLYING?

Cyberbullying occurs when a person uses information technology (IT) to embarrass, harass, intimidate, threaten, or otherwise cause harm to others. Cyberbullying amounts to a technological extension of physical bullying that has traditionally been carried out face to face or indirectly over the telephone, through written messages, or more simply through physical violence. More recently, people have been known to bully other people online by using IT devices. Cyber-stalking is similar to cyberbullying. The main differences between these forms of cyberabuse is that whereas in cyberbullying the perpetrator is known to the victim and usually involves adolescents, in cyberstalking the perpetrator is usually an adult who intends to remain unknown and who usually has more sinister motives, often sexual in nature.

The Internet and World Wide Web have changed bullying and stalking. Desktop and laptop computers, cell phones, electronic gaming devices, and other mobile computing devices have all assisted bullies in transmitting their messages to victims or getting others to join in on bullying once it has started. Today bullies and stalkers can abuse and spy on people online and in-person in ways that may cause even more harm despite being easier to commit and requiring less courage and risk than traditional face-to-face forms of such abuse. Nevertheless, traditional (face-to-face) bullying and (physical) stalking still occur as extensions of the technological kinds of abuse or crime.

The ability to communicate messages using the Internet at any time from either public or private places breaks down boundaries. In addition, asymmetric messaging means that messages can be sent electronically at one time of day so as to ambush a victim when they discover it later online. Small IT devices and the ability to send messages anonymously combine to aid bullies in concealing mean messages they send. Today a bully using a small mobile computing device can simply send a harassing text message (equipped with graphic images and sound) while they are in class to a victim in another classroom or school building without teachers ever becoming aware of what is occurring. The reality of cyberbullying is that bullying communications can be made privately but read, shared, and even broadcast publically.

The word *bullying* brings to mind images of being made fun of on a school bus or playground. Bullying may involve something as simple as a glaring look, or being deliberately bumped in a school hallway, or something more severe like a punch to the face. Regardless of the motives involved, bullying occurs when someone intentionally harasses, intimidates, embarrasses, or threatens one or more people. It usually happens over a period of time and becomes worse if it is not stopped. It can be done by an individual or a group.

Cyberbullying consists of threats, harassment, intimidation, or intentional embarrassment delivered or caused online. As with traditional bullying, cyberbullying usually occurs over a period of time, may involve one or more individual offenders, and is likely to become worse if not stopped.[2]

Most people have experienced something they consider to be bullying or cyberbullying at least once in their lives, whether by a classmate, or even by a family member, teacher, or coworker. Regardless of the form it comes in or who it comes from, bullying always causes harm to its victims. Harm caused by bullies can be emotional, mental, or physical and can also result in property damage.

Bullying may—but does not necessarily—involve criminal activity, even though people are harmed as a result. For example, attempting to kill someone is a crime that causes harm even if the victim does not die, but few people would argue that the person who did this was merely a "bully." However, if someone kicked, shoved, or punched someone else, or threatened them, these actions might be crimes (e.g., assault) depending on circumstances, and they may also be evidence of bullying, especially if they occurred separately over a period of time.

Even though bullying occurs over time it tends to go unnoticed or "flies under the radar" of authorities such as teachers and police officers. This is because authorities need to pay attention to many serious things and do not always realize that bullying is happening or that even when observed, it may be having serious effects on its victims. Bullies often use this to their advantage by committing small acts that cause just enough harm to affect their victim but avoid catching the attention of an adult. With a quick shove or an angry glare, a bully or group of bullies can seriously upset someone, especially when this occurs several times over a period of weeks or months.

When it comes to children, adults often assume bullying implies that the harm caused is somehow not serious. Describing kids that do significant harm to others as "bullies" sometimes implies that as children they "don't know any better." However, even young children understand that being mean to people in-person or online is not nice and wrong and therefore something they should not do. Still, young bullies, when they are caught, often receive less harsh punishment than older kids who are assumed to know better. So whereas young bullies are sent to a principal's office or perhaps suspended from school (especially in cases of serious or repeated bullying), criminals of any age who are found to have bullied in the course of their crime(s) (e.g., assault by punching, kicking, or shoving) may be suspended from school *and* given probation or sent to jail.

Unfortunately bullying is too often regarded as a natural part of life and growing up. Some people dismiss it, saying, after all, "everyone does it" or it "helps toughen people up." Sentiments like these statements often confuse and frustrate victims of bullying into thinking that the harm they are experiencing is normal and not worth reporting to authorities. In severe cases victims feel isolated and trapped, afraid in school or even afraid to go online to socialize.

Many victims also think that reporting bullying when it occurs will not change things and might only make matters worse. The low priority sometimes given to bullying means authorities might not intervene, leaving victims to endure pain and in the constant fear of reprisals for having spoken out. Even adults in the workplace experience similar issues when confronting or reporting abusive coworkers or managers. In these cases reporting may simply signal to an unchecked bully that what he is doing is actually harming the victim as intended, thereby reinforcing the bully's motivations to attack over and over again. All of these reasons—circumstances in which bullying occurs, levels of seriousness of harm caused, lack of responsiveness to "little things" that do not seem worth the attention of authorities, and so on—make identifying or admitting to being bullied and reporting it tricky for victims. Consequently bullying tends to be a label for many different kinds of abuse for which an abuser may go unpunished or receive less punishment than deserved. Therefore bullying might also broadly be defined as: the willful infliction of mental, emotional, or physical harm on another person, often in relatively smaller incidents over a period of time, dispensed in a method that prevents the victim from reporting the abuse to authorities. Here again motives about why bullying occurs is not material to the definition of what it is. Bullies do what they do for all sorts of reasons. Cyberbullying would be the same thing but done online through chat, blogs, e-mail, Web sites, and so forth.

WHAT IS CYBERSTALKING?

Cyberstalking occurs when people use the Internet and information technology (IT) devices, such as computers or cell phones, to send or post harassing messages of an intimidating, threatening, or sexual nature over extended periods of time. Despite the fact that bullying and stalking can often overlap, relatively few people claim they have been victims of stalking. Sometimes the word *stalking* is used as part of a joke to describe anyone who follows someone around too much. The term can also bring to mind a socially awkward person repeatedly asking someone out on a date or the creepy feeling a person gets when a stranger knows too much information about them.

Stalking incidents are rarely clear-cut. Often the line between creepy stalking and romantic or friendly gestures can simply be whether or not the recipient appreciates what the person making the gesture is doing. Even something seemingly innocent can be potentially harmful or scary to the person being followed and contacted. However, these gestures do not constitute stalking when done for official purposes.

Law enforcement officials associate stalking with following someone secretly and harming or frightening him. Legally speaking, stalking involves the willful, malicious, and repeated following and harassing of another person. In this sense, "harassing" is not the same as "bullying" and is used instead to describe any form of repeated attempts at unwanted contact with the person targeted whether or not the attempts include any messages that might be considered offensive. In addition, "following" can be broadly understood to be any form of unwanted information-gathering or spying in addition to actual tracking or chasing.

The overall effect of stalking is that victims feel their privacy is violated and they are afraid for their safety. In some cases the "maliciousness" of stalking comes from the fact that attention is unwanted by the victim, or at least would be if he became aware he was being spied on. However, many stalkers gain considerable pleasure from secretly following their victims without any intention of causing them harm. Indeed they might lose satisfaction if they were discovered.

Again, there is often a very fine line between romance and being overly infatuated with a person, or knowing too much about a person versus stalking them. This usually depends on the perspective of the person being romanced or stalked. If someone does not cease their activities after being asked to stop, the distinction is much easier to make. Quite simply, anyone who has been asked to stop following, contacting, or spying on a person and continues to do so is a stalker.

Like bullying, stalking is nothing new, and stalkers have used various tools and methods to collect information about their victims and to follow them around. Before the widespread use of computing technologies, stalkers gained information through word of mouth or accessing other types of information. For example, if a stalker and victim both worked at the same pizza shop, the stalker could check the victim's work schedule and deduce the times when the victim might be at home. With that information, a stalker might follow a victim home from work, or break into his house while he is away, or simply attempt to change work schedules so that the two would work at the same time. Small bits of information—a home address, a last name, likes and dislikes—can often be combined to lead a stalker to more sensitive information, allowing them to gain more access to a victim and potentially control aspects of their lives.

There is at least one form of stalking that does not immediately lead to a feeling of fear or discomfort in a victim, although it usually is against the law from the start and is connected to crimes that go beyond cyberstalking—predatory grooming. These cases commonly involve a younger victim and an older "predator" who is "grooming" them for sexual activities. Age differences are often precisely why such incidents are considered criminal rather than romantic activity, as local, state, and federal laws forbid sexual contact between adults and minors. One who engages in predatory grooming online would be considered a cyberpredator.

WHY DO CYBERSTALKING AND CYBERBULLYING MATTER?

If cyberstalking and cyberbullying are simply the act of using IT to extend the reach of bullying and stalking, then what makes it different? Why should anyone care about high-tech means of these forms of abuse more than traditional methods?

First, it certainly appears as if cyberbullying, and potentially cyberstalking, are on the rise. Various research studies indicate that about one in three school-aged children admit to being mean online or have experienced someone being mean to them.[2] Media reports also abound with stories of cyberbullying. Some cases involve dozens of offenders and truly traumatized victims, such as with Ryan Halligan.

Second, cyberbullying disrupts school learning environments, which is a major reason why courts have increasingly stepped in to rule that school officials have a responsibility to act on behalf of

Due to an increase in bullying via text messaging and the Internet, schools across the country are confiscating cell phones from students. *(Source: Mike Fuentes/Chicago Tribune/MCT via Getty Images)*

all students by cracking down on the activities of cyberbullies even when their actions take place off of school grounds and after school hours. It follows that the federal government and numerous state governments have recently enacted anti-cyberstalking and cyberbullying laws.

Third, many parents of victims have campaigned for awareness of cyberbullying problems locally and nationally. All of the reporting and discussion makes cyberbullying *appear* as if it is a growing problem for everyone, but that could simply be because cyberbullying is a fairly new phenomenon. Even if there is not an increasing amount of cyberbullying, the use of IT as an extension of traditional bullying has consequences that potentially increase the amount of harm caused to victims.

Fourth, as discussed earlier in the chapter, an increased audience can often lead to more harmful bullying incidents, as more people join in bullying or are exposed to someone's private or embarrassing information. The Internet provides an unprecedented ability to publicize and disseminate information, allowing one person to speak to extremely large audiences very quickly and inexpensively. So, where traditional bullying attempts are usually limited to smaller groups, like a school district or office building, cyberbullying can quickly expand across entire communities and literally throughout the world.

Fifth, anonymity offered by many Internet communications methods allows bullies to avoid detection. Not only does this make bullies who are reported much more difficult to identify and punish, it also makes it easier for others to join in the bullying with reduced or little fear of being caught. With freely available instant messaging accounts and social networking profiles, it can be simple for a bully to post harmful information under a false name or fake account. In fact, bullies can even pretend to be the victim, doing embarrassing things in their name online as a means to cause harm.

Finally, cyberbullying often remains a legal gray area that is too small or inconsequential for a school district or law enforcement agency to investigate in depth. Even when an incident clearly warrants further action, there is often a question of who is responsible for an investigation and how to impose punishment on bullies. Cyberstalking and cyberbullying can be conducted from anywhere there is a computer terminal or Internet connection—from home, school, an office, or while people are on the go using mobile devices. If a student bullies another student, but does it from home, is the school responsible for punishing the bully, or are the parents? Often the answer depends on where the bullying took place or in determining the extent to which entire school learning environments are compromised. As a result, there has been an explosion of discussion and policy making in states and school districts across the nation, with everyone trying to work out how best to deal with the problem of cyberbullying.

INFORMATION FOUND IN THIS BOOK

This book is about cyberstalking and cyberbullying—an irksome and too often harmful combination of online behaviors brought about by causing fear in people singled out for abuse. Cyberbullying is mostly done by young users of information technology devices and the Internet against other young users who are disliked or being picked on for some reason. Cyberbullying usually involves a lead bully and piling on by other kids who become involved in both online and off-line bullying activities.

Cyberstalking involves online spying and is mostly done by adults against other adults, either because victims are adored or hated by the individual responsible. As with cyberbullying, cyberstalking can involve off-line as well as online activities that cause fear, anger, and depression in victims affected.

Chapter 1 explains why people are mean to each other online. Emphasized here is the reality that people are not born mean, but unfortunately can make poor choices when they are using IT devices and the Internet.

Chapter 2 describes who bullies and stalks people online. Demographic differences among sex and age of bullies and stalkers is explained with regard to social, economic, and educational status of offenders and relationships they have with victims.

Chapter 3 discusses behavioral tactics bullies and stalkers use.

Chapter 4 lists and discusses technological methods of cyberstalking and cyberbullying.

Chapter 5 describes what it is like to be bullied or stalked online and the many kinds of harmful consequences that victims must endure.

Chapter 6 reviews what police, school officials, and parents are doing and should do even more in order to stop cyberstalking and cyberbullying.

Chapter 7 explains how people can avoid and prevent cyberstalking and cyberbullying, primarily by being alert for and reporting abuse when they experience it, by standing up for their rights, and by choosing to be a good cybercitizen.

CONCLUSION

Cyberstalking and cyberbullying are similar forms of online abuse. They sometimes lead to horrific results, including physical injury and even suicide. The story of Ryan Halligan is only one example among many disturbing stories that reflect the experiences of many Internet users.

Keep in mind that the horrific stories discussed here are examples of highly publicized cases, and that a majority of circumstances and problems that victims of online abuse face are smaller incivilities inflicted upon them and thousands of other people like them every day. Remember that if you are a victim, you are not alone and help is available.

While disturbing, cyberstalking and cyberbullying should also be regarded as real and potential problems that users of the Internet may become involved in however unintentionally. Even so, information technology including the Internet and devices, such as computers and cell phones, are important means of communication necessary in computerized societies. As such the challenge is to learn where online dangers lurk so as to promote cybersafety and cybersecurity in the daily lives and online interactions of users everywhere.

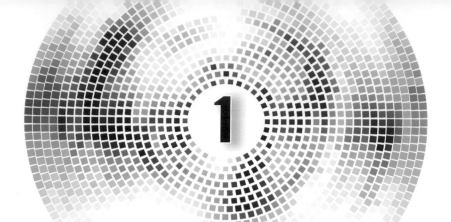

Why Are People Mean to Each Other Online?

Kevin is 14 years old and, because he was held back for a year, is still in seventh grade. He is tall and more developed than his classmates. Everyone "just knows" he takes medicine to control his attention deficit disorder and anger. Most of the kids at school shun Kevin, who is a known bully. He spends time with a few other bullies who talk tough and like to pick on good students or those who wear nice clothes or kids who are computer geeks or weak athletes. Glares, intentional bumping and tripping in hallways, name-calling, and even following "good kids" home after school to intimidate them are common activities for Kevin and his friends, who take their lead from him, as if to gain his approval. In school and in surrounding neighborhoods when school is not in session they are the bullies who instill fear.

Kevin was not born a bully, nor was he destined to become one. His mean-spirited ways came about over time as he experienced academic difficulty and was himself bullied by other students for being "stupid." Many elementary school subjects like English, math, and *history were not easy for Kevin to learn. Reading was also difficult for him, so he had trouble understanding subjects addressed in books and found other kinds of reading assignments to be confusing. He simply could not grasp much beyond general concepts. Consequently he was reluctant to speak up or answer questions in class. His grades on assignments and in courses were often below average. His teachers tried to help, but the school district he attended was poorly resourced and not able to provide the special education program assistance that Kevin really needed. In time other students regarded him as "slow" or "dense" or "stupid" and they called him these things.*

As it happened Kevin was always big for his age. When he was held back a year in school, his physical size in comparison to his classmates made him appear even bigger, which of course he was. This led to snide comments about his size and other maturing characteristics such as growing facial hair. Even though he was only in seventh grade, Kevin was already shaving. While showering after gym class, less mature students were amazed by the amount and thickness of his body hair. So in addition to comments about his marginal performance in classes, students also made fun of his physical appearance. "Gee, I wonder what Paul Bunyan scored on his exam? He should just live in the forest and swing an axe for a living. He's never going to amount to anything."

The story about Kevin supports mainstream social science, and criminology theories that, in general, people are not born or destined to grow up mean. Instead people tend to learn right from wrong in early childhood. As they age most people develop a sense of morality and a sense for choosing proper things to do on the basis of customary standards of behavior prevalent within their community. Although individual communities may have different standards of behavior governing specific things, larger society understands and accepts general principles about what is right or wrong. For example, stealing things and beating up people is simply wrong and against the law.

Children usually imitate the behaviors of their parents and other adults who they respect. As children become older they learn to set good examples for their younger brothers and sisters. If sound parenting and positive role modeling is not present in a child's life, she is more prone to imitate poor and harmful behaviors such as cyberbullying or cyberstalking.

In general people choose to do right things like being kind to people less fortunate, or they chose to do wrong things such as bully or stalk other people. Decisions about how to behave in various situations are normally made on the basis of learning what will be rewarded versus being punished. Ideally positive behaviors come to dominate potentially harmful behaviors so that children (and adults) do not become prone to misbehaving and harming other people.

Young people who engage in bullying may lack adult guidance, positive role models, or the ability to distinguish right from wrong. *(Source: © John Birdsall/The Image Works)*

IT DEVICES AND DISSOCIATION THEORY

Another important factor that relates to making proper decisions not to engage in cyberbullying or cyberstalking involves dissociation theory and what some researchers and activists refer to as the Online Disinhibition Effect.[1] These terms refer to what happens when people need not immediately face the consequences of their actions, such as in the online world. A person who feels safer bullying online rather than face-to-face is experiencing dissociation. Dissociation occurs when circumstances limit or minimize human interactions, as when a person uses a computer and the Internet to bully someone or spy on her. In effect, dissociation means that bullies find it easier to "hide behind" the screen of their IT device rather than confront a victim in person.

For a long time, research has confirmed that circumstances, including those created by technological media, that distance abusers from understanding or feeling the pain they cause other people, has a reinforcing effect that results in their being more likely to repeat their harmful actions. Think of it like this: When people are allowed to get away with bullying online they learn to bully more, and probably in more ways, over time. Left uncorrected, bullies become even meaner.

There are a few researchers, however, who claim that while people are not born to be mean, they may be born with certain biological characteristics that impair their ability to be loving, affectionate, or take direction from authority figures. In fact, some crime researchers believe that a person's physical characteristics coupled with her social and economic circumstances and behavioral choices compound in ways that contribute to personality and a propensity to behave in ways that do or do not cause harm.

An important aspect of this theory rests on a person's ability to distinguish right from wrong behavior. Children or mentally disturbed people sometimes have difficulty distinguishing right from wrong behavioral choices. These are complex issues for which there are not simple answers. Even so, all people deserve to be treated with respect. This applies even to people who make mistakes and are willing to correct their actions.

ONLINE ABUSE IS NOT "NORMAL"

Many people, including parents of bullying victims, who have themselves experienced bullying, believe it is only natural and normal for kids to bully each other. People who hold this mistaken belief may also believe several other myths about bullying and cyberbullying, such as:[2]

1. "Bullying helps victims 'toughen up' and only makes them stronger in the long run."
2. "Bullying is sometimes playing or goofing around, so what's the big deal?"
3. "When bullying becomes serious enough, kids will tell an adult."

In reality, bullying hurts, and left unchecked, causes serious pain. Bullying is not playing around. In addition, "youth rarely tell parents or other adults about being bullied. This is especially true if their friends are the bullies. Instead [victims of bullying] live by a code of silence with 'no snitching' allowed."[3] Bullying in all its forms (i.e., intentional harassment, intimidation, embarrassment, or threats) is a very serious problem. Whether bullying occurs face to face and/or online, bullying causes distress and depression among its victims. So does cyberstalking.

Abuse occurs through the actions of people when they have malicious intentions and are disrespectful toward another person. Disrespect occurs in many ways, such as calling someone names, talking behind their back, offending as through physical attack, stalking, and so forth. All these and many other forms of disrespect involve different, but frequently overlapping, forms of behavior and motivations. For example, a person who has been bullied online may feel angry and spiteful as she posts mean messages to a Facebook page about someone who offended her. And while it is normal to initially feel angry or spiteful when offended, actually following through on impulses to offend in return or to adopt an offending personality, attitude, or lifestyle is not normal or acceptable. Of course not being mean in return for having been offended online is sometimes easier said than done, especially when IT devices are right in hand. After all, most cyberstalking and cyberbullying that takes place goes largely unnoticed by anyone except the abuser and the victim, so a mean message sent via text or an angry comment posted on someone's wall is not likely to go any further. But is that really true?

The convenience of devices and instant messaging and texting requires that responsible users pause, think, and then react to a disrespectful message so as not to stir up further trouble. It is better to confront someone who upsets one online in a face-to-face conversation rather than fire off a rapid message designed to fan the proverbial flames.

Unfortunately, with so many people possessing IT devices, thoughtless and even intentionally abusive messages have become part of everyday life on the Internet for many users. When hurtful messages are not clarified, retracted, or apologized for, hurt feelings mount over time, increasing strains between people who are ordinarily friends or at least could get along were it not for an electronic spat.

Once offensive messages are posted and responded to, spats often gain wider and wider audiences as friends are copied in on distribution lists. Before a user knows it, an argument has ensued and been made public through widespread posting on the Internet. And with so many people possessing IT devices and tempted to comment on anything and everything that may have anything to do with them or someone they know, mean posts and texts are quickly perpetuated. Sometimes friends of one or the other people in the spat join in on the abuse.

Given the ubiquitous nature of IT, victims seeking revenge or escape from piling-on attacks often feel as if there is no escape from the torment they feel. Physical or face-to-face abuse at school or work, once started, spreads like an uncontrolled forest fire, leaving only emotional ashes behind continued messaging via cell phones and the Internet.

In a sense, IT has allowed for larger scales of online abuse, with larger public visibility, larger groups of attackers, and wider ranges of times and locations from which hurtful messages can be sent and received. What IT has not done, however, is to fundamentally change the nature of abuse, which remains abnormal in societies comprised mainly of good people who may periodically make a mistake by sending a mean text or e-mail. So while IT devices and the Internet have made it more common for hurtful or offensive messages to be made and easier for anonymous and intentional attackers to abuse people, most victims of abuse, whether it be online or off-line, know their attackers. This allows them to figure out their attacker's intentions if they take time to pause and think before posting. Think of it like this: People who have never met usually do not start spontaneously sending nasty messages to one another—they have to meet and interact with each other first, even if their meeting is only online. As such, there is often a layered quality to instances of bullying or stalking, where a face-to-face meeting can spark verbally abusive cell phone conversations, harassing messages on social networking sites and instant messenger, and the posting of embarrassing or inappropriate material online. This, in turn, allows time to defuse a situation if users pause and think through the possible consequences of what they are about to send.

Ryan Halligan's case is just one example where messages got out of control. He had trouble with groups of bullies inside of school, trouble that eventually led to physical bullying, which later spread to online harassment, including a girl pretending to be interested

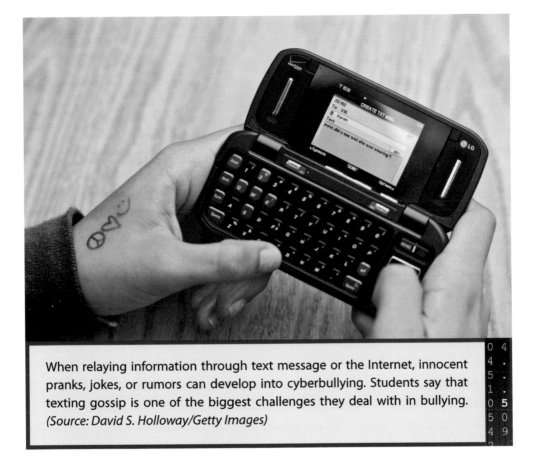

When relaying information through text message or the Internet, innocent pranks, jokes, or rumors can develop into cyberbullying. Students say that texting gossip is one of the biggest challenges they deal with in bullying. *(Source: David S. Holloway/Getty Images)*

in dating him. Eventually an online "friend" encouraged him to kill himself. News flash: This is not normal or acceptable! These and other online forms of abuse are serious and, although relatively new, can only be understood within the context of more traditional forms of bullying and stalking.

Online versions of bullying and stalking committed by and among children, teenagers, and adults often involve complicated personal relationships and issues. For example, some cyberbullying may involve spying on and therefore stalking a victim to learn how they are reacting to insults or threats. In addition, cyberstalking and cyberbullying are forms of online abuse that often, though not always, rise to the level of being criminal in nature. These are extremely challenging problems for society to address.

BULLYING OR STALKING IS ABOUT HAVING POWER OVER OTHERS

If cyberstalking and cyberbullying causes harm, why does anyone do it and even enjoy bullying or stalking? Most people consider themselves to be "good people" who would not intentionally hurt others. In fact, there can be unintentional bullying. A simple joke or prank to one person can be offensive and harmful to another person—it all depends on perspective. Usually it is far more amusing, and therefore enjoyable, to be the initiator of a joke rather than the target of one. However, saying "I didn't mean any harm" is no excuse for anyone, including bullies or stalkers who often know perfectly well when they are hurting someone.

Consider that even when an ordinarily pleasant person who is not a bully plays a prank or joke on someone, she knows it is or could be somewhat hurtful. Still a jokester makes fun and enjoys herself even at the expense of others. Poking fun at others or pulling pranks for "entertainment" just "because I thought it would be funny" is all too common. It is not surprising then that the word *bullying* may apply to any infliction of harm against others regardless of motivations involved. This includes playing small pranks and jokes, whether the motive is envy, revenge, anger, to impress one's peers, respond to a dare, or whatever.

Regardless of motivations, circumstances, and the form and amount of harm caused by bullying, all incidents of bullying have one thing in common: power. Establishing and maintaining feelings of power over someone else feels good to bullies, who enjoy dominating other people. Having power over the actions and beliefs of others is also necessary, however, for parents, teachers, and other adults who need to be in control and be good role models. What is the difference?

Power is difficult to explain because it has positive and negative connotations depending on how and why it is used. Establishing and maintaining power generally pertains to the position of authority or influence that exists between individuals in a relationship.

Having power over someone should involve: (a) having acknowledged and appropriate levels of authority, (b) being a person capable of acting responsibly in normal and even emergency circumstances, and (c) actually being and feeling responsible for another person that one "is in charge of." For example, parents have legal and natural authority over their children and are responsible for their care and well-being. Similarly an older brother or sister may naturally feel responsible for younger siblings, unless he or she has special needs and in which case a younger sibling may be given and exercise power in the relationship.

Unfortunately some people misunderstand or misuse power, as is evident when they think or say things like "I'm better than you" and mean it. Bullies often think to themselves in these terms: "I'm powerful enough to do this to you, and you're too powerless to stop me." Bullying someone in front of others sends the same message to witnesses of bullying behavior. If witnesses are friends with the bully, more and more bullying often occurs. Piling on occurs when others want to share the power and status of a bully. In their mistaken belief, they certainly do not want to be known as a loser or like the person who is being bullied.

People tempted into piling on may think "it seemed like fun" or "everyone was doing it." But what those who claim "everyone was doing it" never admit is that everyone except the victim was having a good time. In this way, bullying is also about exclusion. By sending the message that the bully is "better than" the victim, victims will naturally feel inferior or become angry. In some cases, especially when victims feel they cannot tell an adult about bullying, they may take matters into their own hands by resorting to revenge and becoming a bully themselves to "get back at" someone.

As more people laugh at, participate in, or ignore bullying instead of stopping it, they and other people will effectively "buy in" and promote bullying as being "not that bad." In so doing they send messages to everyone that bullying is okay. The short-term consequence is that bullies feel more empowered to increase the frequency

POWER OVER VICTIMS IN STALKING AND BULLYING

Many principles and processes in bullying, including those relating to power, apply also to stalking. Cyberstalkers seek power over their victims but do so in secretive ways by spying on them. Stalkers generally act alone rather than with friends, and there is no piling-on effect. There are far fewer stalkers than bullies, and because their spying activities are mysterious and sinister, they derive power mainly by perpetuating fantasies about relationships they would like to have with their victim(s). For stalkers, power is also achieved through direct, observable actions that cause fear of future name-calling, shoving, threats, actually being assaulted, and so forth; or by instilling fear of the unknown, which victims worry about or dwell on.

Since bullies and stalkers both seek to establish and maintain power over their victims, they are actually just malicious people who employ different strategies. Logically the same would apply to cyberstalking and cyberbullying, in which offenders use the Internet and IT devices to dominate others through power instilled by fear.

and intensity of their bullying, and to expand the number of people and locations of their bullying. The larger and longer-term consequence is that bullying is extended and reinforced throughout communities. This in turn causes myths about bullying being acceptable, which only worsens what victims of bullying experience. Vicious spirals of bullying will persist until they are stopped.

CAN PEOPLE LEARN TO GET ALONG AND RESPECT ONE ANOTHER?

Can people learn to get along and respect one another? Of course they can! The fact that most people do get along in schools, in churches, and while playing and working with each other in communities throughout the world is evidence that people prefer to get along. People also most certainly can learn to get along even if they do not really like each other. This is a matter of being mature and practical because things like bullying and stalking, and therefore cyberstalking and cyberbullying, cost too much for individuals involved and for the communities in which they live. The challenge is learning how to avoid, put up with, or stop cyberstalking and cyberbullying before it becomes a problem. This is not always easy and has much to do with understanding who is prone to engaging in these inappropriate behaviors.

CONCLUSION

People are mean to each other frequently because they seek power over others who seem weaker or inferior in some way. Cyberbullies and cyberstalkers gain power by instilling fear in their victims. Power acquired through hurting others is learned behavior and likely to be repeated to the extent people are successful and feel rewarded rather than punished for having gotten away with their online conduct.

Bullies and bullying beget more of the same. Piling on occurs as witnesses to bullying choose to engage in more bullying of a particular person or group of people. Piling on often happens as people seek to be associated with or receive approval from the person who started bullying in the first place. When bullying and piling on are not stopped, they recur and spread within schools and throughout neighborhoods. The hyper-connected world of information sharing, made possible and inevitable by the Internet, makes it necessary for all users to pause and think before sending online messages.

Whereas most bullies incur friends who are willing or eager to imitate their bullying, stalkers act secretly and alone to gain power over people by instilling fear, primarily of the unknown. Stalkers specialize in spying on people and lurking around to observe their actions. As they experience greater need for power, they may leave threatening messages or even clues about their identity.

Who Bullies and Stalks People Online?

Not all cyberstalking cases involve "creepy" older men and underage girls. Adults can also be targets of cyberstalking, often with damaging results, as Chester Charles Bennington—the lead singer for the Grammy Award-winning band Linkin Park—and his wife found out. In March 2006, his wife, Talinda, aged 29, found a strange e-mail in her inbox. She and Chester had only been married a short time when they received an e-mail that contained a simple message congratulating the couple. The tone of the e-mail was less than friendly, however, as it linked to the personal Web page of Chester's then ex-wife.

In the next month, another message was received from an ex-boyfriend of Talinda's, who had himself received a strange message discussing their past relationship. Later, while Chester was out of town, Talinda received a strangely threatening e-mail referencing how difficult it must be to be alone. Talinda suspected someone familiar with her background was spying on her.

Eventually Chester began to receive eerily silent calls on his private cell phone in the early morning. Daily calls once totaled 15, but each time revealed only a blocked caller ID. Once, when Talinda answered one of the calls, a woman's voice said simply, "I'm watching you."

As the Benningtons struggled to ignore the strange messages, assuming them to be the work of a few particularly irritating fans, even more e-mail messages began to arrive from friends, asking about a series of strange messages that had appeared to originate from Talinda's account. The spying was becoming more technically complicated as revealed by the ability of the stalker(s) to somehow take control of the Bennington's computer.

As the summer arrived, Talinda discovered someone had hacked the password to her eBay account and was actively attempting to do the same to her PayPal account. The same thing happened to Chester's Verizon wireless cell phone account. At that point the Benningtons contacted police who, unfortunately and mistakenly told them, that under existing laws investigation was not possible until the Benningtons were physically assaulted.

Unsatisfied, Chester and Talinda hired a private investigator who specialized in digital forensics. But the couple became increasingly paranoid, trusting only each other while suspecting friends and even family members of possibly stalking them! Next the couple purchased an alarm system and a guard dog. The cyberstalking continued, however, with taunting messages about the location of the Bennington's children.

It had been more than a year since the original e-mails were received and the Benningtons were more worried than ever. By then the private investigator had developed a significant amount of information about the online stalker. He determined that all of the messages had originated in New Mexico. Slowly amassing evidence by picking through the electronic details in the messages, he uncovered a trail that pointed to a woman named Devon Townsend. According to her MySpace page, Townsend, in 2009, was the mother of a *one-year-old child and worked at Sandia National Labs—a nuclear weapons research facility—as a computer technician with access to government security clearances. Because of the sensitive nature of the stalker's employment, the case was immediately referred to federal law enforcement agents, who took a keen interest in the case.*

Agents arrested Townsend, who described how she had easily guessed the password to Chester Bennington's e-mail account after seeing it appear on a mass-e-mail. (He had simply used his middle name "Charlie" to protect his private messages.) When asked why she had stalked the couple, she stated that she wanted to be closer to the band, especially Chester, "to part of what he is." In reaction to the arrest, Chester said, "I don't go out and pick fights, but when you find out some total stranger has personal pictures of your kids in the bath, has phone numbers of your parents and close friends and every business associate...it fuels my desire to make sure this kind of action is viewed as criminal." Townsend was later sentenced to two years in prison for cyberstalking the Benningtons.[1]

On any given day most students walking through school hallways can point out the school bullies. Whether they have been picked on or not, students often know the people who are trying to make innocent people feel bad. In general, bullies are believed to be more aggressive toward their peers and often to adults such as parents and teachers. Bullies usually have an apathetic attitude toward hurting others and therefore do not take into consideration how their negative actions affect their victims. Many, but not all bullies, are also insecure about themselves, have anger management issues, and take their frustrations out on other people.

Take, for instance, a school's athletic star. She may attract the popular boys and have the support of all the athletic students in school. As a superstar athlete, she might be tempted to believe she is superior to others in ways beyond her athletic talent. She might bully nonathletes or even other athletes who are smaller or weaker than her. After all, a star does not necessarily care about the feelings of others. However, this is not the case with most student athletes.

Chester Bennington and his family were victims of cyberstalking for more than a year. During that time, the cyberstalker read their personal e-mail and used their accounts to contact their family and friends. *(Source: AP Photo/ Tammie Arroyo)*

CHARACTERISTICS OF BULLIES AND THEIR VICTIMS

Bullies and stalkers tend to be older than their victims. Bullies naturally dominate younger people, whereas stalkers envy younger victims and can more easily manipulate them. Both bullies and stalkers need to feel more powerful and superior to their victims. Conversely, victims of bullies and stalkers can often be identified by the lack of supportive peer relationships, lack of confidence in interacting with others, and generally being more passive.[2] For example, an eighth grader might pick on a sixth grader just starting out in a new middle school. Being the "new kid" in school can be challenging enough with having to adapt to a new environment, new teachers, and new rules. "Newbies" are easy targets because they have few friends at first and have not figured out groups of people they feel comfortable hanging out with for support. When they are picked on, it is hard for them to find support among fellow classmates because many students may already be inclined to support and pile onto the antics of a bully.

Bullies also tend to violate rules and get into trouble. As referenced in one book about cyberbullying, "Those who bully are more likely to get into physical fights, damage and steal property, drop out of school and carry a weapon. Also of significance, bullies are more likely to report owning guns that are used for intimidation. In addition, bullies have also been associated with groups who systematically victimize specific groups of peers and boys identified as bullies are four times more likely to have a criminal conviction by age 24."[3]

Gender and Age

Research about the online behaviors of youth reveal that kids start being mean to each other on the Internet as early as seven and eight years of age, when they are in second grade. Furthermore, boys are mean online earlier in life than girls are. However, by middle school age, girls are more likely to engage in cyberbullying than boys are, a trend that does not change until high school years and afterward.[4] Research also reveals that older teenage girls are more engaged in interpersonal communications and wider online topical-information searching than similarly aged boys. In addition, males are more likely to be bullied by other males, while females are bullied by males and females in nearly equal numbers. Finally, and in reference to the online and off-line aspects of bullying, younger and adolescent males are more likely to be physically bullied than their female counterparts. However, adolescent girls are more likely to be victims of rumors and sexual comments, whether these occur online or off-line.[5]

Social, Economic and Education Factors

Social, economic, and education factors can play a big part in child and adolescent misbehavior. Law enforcement and juvenile justice

BEING MEAN ONLINE
OFTEN BEGINS EARLY

Computerization along with ease of accessing an ever-expanding World Wide Web has led to kids increasingly using the Internet earlier in life. In 2007–2008, Dr. Samuel C. McQuade and his colleagues completed a major study of Internet and at-risk behaviors of youth.[6] Of 4,700 kindergarten and first-grade students surveyed in 2007–2008, 51 percent reported that they use a home computer to access the Internet for Web browsing, communicating with other people, and playing online games. Similarly, of 5,500 second and third graders surveyed, 67 percent reported having Internet access from some location not limited to their home, and by using a variety of electronic devices, including computers, cell phones, home video game consoles, and/or portable video game consoles. Fully 94 percent of these students reported they engage in online gaming.

Oftentimes young children are not closely supervised in their online activities and interactions with other people. Yet researchers were surprised to learn that 18 percent of second- and third-grade students reported that someone had been mean to them online within the last school year. In addition, 9 percent of these students admitted they had been mean to someone online within the same time period.

These statistics reveal that cyberbullying is experienced early in life for many computer users either as victims of bullying, as bullies, or both. The implication is that guidance and supervision provided by parents and older siblings, along with teachers in educational settings, and other respected adults, are essential for kids to remain safe, secure, and responsible in their own social computing activities.

administrators commonly call attention to these factors in describing why kids commit crimes. When it comes to cyberstalking and cyberbullying, however, demographic circumstances matter very little, if at all. A bully is a bully regardless of how much money her family has, what her race or ethnicity is, or what sex she is. Yet, being different in any of these ways or other ways can increase the likelihood of being singled out. A child whose family is poor and wears old clothes but attends school in a rather wealthy school district may be picked on merely because her parents have little money and are not able to buy nice things. The same is true for people who are very pretty, particularly talented, wear glasses (especially at an early age), and so forth. Anything that makes a person stand out may give reason for her to be bullied or stalked.

Relationships Between Abusers and Their Victims

In 2005, researchers at the Crimes Against Children Research Center of the University of New Hampshire repeated a major study of online abuse experienced by youth. In this study 1,500 Internet users between the ages of 10 and 17 were interviewed on the phone. Sixty percent reported they did not know who bullied them online, but 40 percent did know their bully and had some type of relationship with them. The study also found that youth were more likely to be bullied online by other youth under the age of 18, in comparison to only 2 percent of cases involving bullies over the age of 25.[7] This means that bullying is more common among children than among adults, and that adults who engage in bullying are more likely to do so as stalkers and remain a mystery to their victims even if they have a relationship with them, which is often the case.

Another major study conducted by the U.S. Department of Justice (DOJ), found that victims are usually stalked or harassed by someone of their own age and race. A majority of stalkers have formed a relationship with their victims, with only one in ten being complete strangers when the stalking took place. One in five stalkers were found to have been in an intimate relationship with their victim; one in seven had been a friend, roommate, or neighbor; and one in ten lived with their victim(s) when the stalking began.[8]

In this same study, male victims of stalking were as likely to be stalked by male or female stalkers, but female victims were more likely to be stalked by male stalkers (in two out of three cases). Four out of ten stalkers were employed and one out of three had been in trouble with the law. The study also determined that the two most common reasons for stalking were anger or spite (in three out of ten cases) or a desire to exert power over a victim (also in three out of ten cases).

HOW MUCH CYBERSTALKING AND CYBERBULLYING OCCURS?

Anyone may become a cyberbully or cyberstalker as the result of many circumstances in their lives. How many cyberbullies and cyberstalkers are there? How "big" are the problems of cyberstalking and cyberbullying? Data gathered by researchers can mean different things depending on how questions are asked and answers interpreted. Even so, sound research has revealed that:

- About 82,000 American adults are estimated to be victims of stalking or harassment. Of these people 20,500 are victims of cyberstalking, and 6,300 are victims of electronic monitoring.[9]
- Approximately one in three young people ages 10–15 years of age have been bullied (i.e., harassed) online; 6 percent know the abuser, and 8 percent report being cyberbullied more than once per month.[10]
- Of teens who report having been cyberbullied, 15 percent report experiencing release of a confidential e-mail, IM, or text message by having it forwarded or posted where others could see it; 13 percent reported having a rumor spread about them online or having someone send them an aggressive or threatening message; and 6 percent reported that someone had posted an embarrassing picture of them online without their permission.[11]
- Within the previous school year: 9 percent of hundreds of second and third graders surveyed reported having been "mean to someone online" and 18 percent reported that

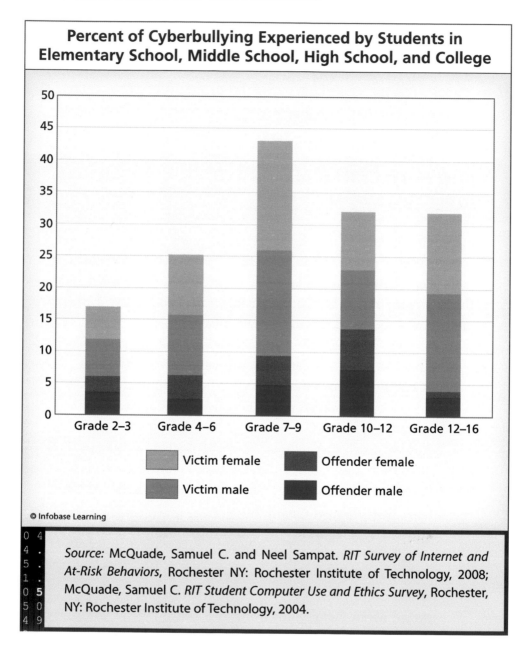

Percent of Cyberbullying Experienced by Students in Elementary School, Middle School, High School, and College

Legend:
- Victim female
- Offender female
- Victim male
- Offender male

© Infobase Learning

Source: McQuade, Samuel C. and Neel Sampat. *RIT Survey of Internet and At-Risk Behaviors*, Rochester NY: Rochester Institute of Technology, 2008; McQuade, Samuel C. *RIT Student Computer Use and Ethics Survey*, Rochester, NY: Rochester Institute of Technology, 2004.

someone online has been mean to them within the last school year; among 8,000 fourth to sixth graders surveyed, 10 percent had been embarrassed and 7 percent had been bullied; of approximately 10,000 seventh- to ninth-grade students surveyed, 15 percent had been embarrassed online, 13 percent had been cyberbullied, and 8 percent had done these things to others online; and of nearly 7,000 tenth to twelfth graders surveyed, 11 percent had been stalked online.[12]

In 2009, the Bureau of Justice Statistics of the U. S. Department of Justice released a special report on stalking, based on a survey of 65,000 crime victims. The resulting report provides a variety of useful statistics on the nature and extent of stalking and harassment in the United States. Of particular note is inclusion of cyberstalking data that involves e-mail, instant messenger, blogs, attack sites, chat rooms, and "electronic monitoring," which included the use of computer recording software, digital video recording, wireless listening devices, and GPS units. The report clearly revealed that one in four of all stalking victims experienced some form of cyberstalking, and only 1 in 13 indicated they had been electronically monitored.[13]

CONCLUSION

Studies about cyberstalking and cyberbullying indicate that these forms of abuse are problematic for many people who use the Internet. Both cyberstalking and cyberbullying strike fear into victims. Offenders, who have problems of their own, too often get away with being mean. At the same time offenders who bully or stalk people online find it easier to accomplish by using computers or other types of IT devices such as cell phones rather than face-to-face communication.

Kids and adults can become offenders or victims of cyberbullying or cyberstalking. The best current evidence shows that boys are more likely than girls to be bullies and to be bullied. Cyberbullying begins as early as kindergarten years. It peaks in middle school possibly only for females, but it remains high with males who dominate as offenders throughout high school and into college.

Younger kids are usually bullied because of their appearance. Middle school and older teens are most often involved in bullying related to sex, sexual orientation, or other relationship issues.

Cyberbullying can be done by a stranger, but is often, if not usually, done by someone known to the victim online and/or in person. Cyberbullies are often also traditional face-to-face bullies, and most cyberbullying victims are also victims of traditional bullying.

Despite risks indicated by this research, users should not be discouraged from going online for fear of bullies or stalkers unless they are already experiencing a problem. Cyberstalking and cyberbullying are problems that deserve attention from adults, including parents, teachers, and law enforcement officials. Nothing indicated by research, however, substantiates that the best way to avoid victimization is to avoid the benefits of the Internet altogether. Despite the fact that cyberstalking and cyberbullying are being treated as new phenomena in society, these problems are rooted in age-old misbehavior that has existed for generations. From this we can deduce that the Internet is not the problem, but people who use it may be problematic.

How People Bully
or Stalk Online

Phoebe Prince moved to Massachusetts from Ireland in the fall of 2009, and nearly immediately found herself to be a victim of numerous bullying incidents by a handful of classmates at South Hadley High School. The bullies appeared to be primarily upset over the fact that Prince had "stolen" an ex-boyfriend of one girl. Phoebe's new relationship was maliciously used as a basis for rumors and insults. She was attacked repeatedly in school, as the bullies screamed insults at her and threatened her with physical violence.[1] Phoebe also faced a significant amount of cyberbullying, primarily through the social networking sites Twitter and Facebook, and via text messaging.

Most of the online bullying involved racial slurs and comments about sexual promiscuity. After three months of the bullying, the bullies drove past Phoebe as she was walking home from school, pelting her with a can of soda and laughing. That afternoon, after a series of texts with one of her friends discussing how difficult school was becoming, she committed suicide.

Initially Phoebe Prince's case appeared to be a classic example of "mean girls" at their worst. In the following days and weeks additional information was revealed through interviews with students at the school Phoebe attended. The interviews revealed that Prince had deliberately attempted to break up relationships of a number of girls at school by spreading rumors that she had been intimate with their boyfriends. This behavior seemingly stemmed from earlier psychological problems that had manifested while Prince was living in Ireland.[2]

In many ways, this case represents not only the damages that are faced by bullying victims—which for Prince was her own life—but additionally by the perpetrators of bullying themselves and the community within which the bullying took place. Six students were indicted by the Massachusetts district attorney on charges related to Prince's suicide. Two of them were boys she had dated during the short months in her new school. These boys were accused of statutory rape, largely on the basis of the rumors that had been circulated by the bullies and by Prince. Of the remaining students who faced criminal charges, three were expelled from South Hadley High School. As the principal told reporters, "These students' lives have also been dramatically altered, and they won't be graduating from South Hadley High School."[3]

The incident gained national media attention and sparked outrage across the country, causing the school itself to come under investigation. Prosecutors attempted to determine whether or not school administrators and teachers had done enough to prevent the daily attacks faced by Prince. In the process numerous students were placed under investigation or otherwise had their studies interrupted. The incident also resulted in emotional loss faced by Phoebe's family, stress faced by the families of the bullies, and thousands of dollars in legal costs spent by families involved. In addition, the state spent large sums, and the reputation of the school district suffered—all the result of one girl being bullied. In the end, cyberbullying continued to be a problem for Prince even after her death, as Internet users defaced a memorial Web page with derogatory comments, eventually leading to closing of the site.

Bullying and cyberbullying are often inseparable, with cyber-bullying acting as yet another means of abuse available to everyday bullies. Furthermore, victims of bullies are often found to have engaged in forms of bullying themselves at some point in their lives. Cyberbullying and stalking can be done by individuals and groups of offenders, and bullies can form into groups to attack their victims. Bullies and stalkers can range in age and can vary in their reasoning as to why they wish to harm their victims. However, even though individuals and groups of offenders might vary, the harmful effects of bullies and stalkers are shared by all victims. Especially tragic cases such as the one involving Phoebe Prince can have far-reaching consequences for families involved, for entire school districts, for a larger community, and even an entire state or nation. Ubiquitous access to the Internet and IT devices create more opportunities for bullying and stalking online. As part of dealing with this phenom-enon, it is necessary to understand the difference between individual and group attacks, how people are targeted for abuse, and how rapid-fire messaging and sly language are used.

IDENTIFYING, CHOOSING, AND TARGETING VICTIMS

By virtue of IT devices and the Internet, cyberstalking and cyberbul-lying can take place anywhere these technologies can be accessed, including from within school classrooms or on school buses, in shopping malls or sporting arenas, and from within homes, cars, or other private and public places. Computing technology has allowed bullies and stalkers to bypass limitations established by geographic boundaries in order to harass, intimidate, threaten, or embarrass their victims. Consequently victimization can occur at any time of day or night from various locations simply depending on tech-nologies and methods used. IT devices and the Internet also allow numerous people to engage in cyberbullying at the same time. Bul-lies and stalkers do not need to even reside in the same community, state, or country as their victim(s) to be effective in causing harm.

The process of offending begins with "identifying" a potential victim. How is this done? Bullies look for victims who are younger, physically smaller, apparently weaker, and more passive than themselves. Bullies also scan for victims who stand out in other ways, such as wearing glasses, having an "odd" haircut, dressing differently, being a particularly bright or struggling student, behaving in a particular way on one or more occasions, or having certain family situations. Even being considered a "geek" or a "nerd," or befriending someone who is, can lead to being bullied.

Since so many kids fit one or more common victim characteristics, the challenge for a bully in "choosing" a target is to find someone, or a small group of people, who possess as many "odd" things as possible in comparison to other potential victims. Frequently a new kid in a school, like Phoebe Prince was, is an easy target because they automatically stand out. Phoebe was very pretty and appears to have engaged in spreading rumors even as rumors were spread about her dating practices. As such Phoebe had three things going against her:

1.   She was new.
2.   She was pretty.
3.   She became involved in rumors about dating, which caught the attention and ire of other kids in school.

The result was an online war of words in which several students engaged in piling on to bully Phoebe. This is not to suggest that Phoebe deserved or asked to be bullied! She did not. This only identifies some of the factors that led to her becoming a victim of bullying.

Once a victim is selected for bullying or for stalking, offenders engage in "targeting" him for frequent harassment. Here the challenge for bullies and stalkers involves determining many personal things about a victim. For example, where a victim lives is important so he can be looked for on their way to or from school. Older student victims who hold jobs are doubly vulnerable because they have *three* places they need to be at depending on the time of day: home, school, or work. It is also important for offenders to discover what IT device(s) and areas of the Internet victims use, such as what online

District Attorney David Sullivan addresses the public after court hearings in Northampton, Massachusetts. The hearings were connected to the death of Phoebe Prince, a victim of bullying. *(Source: AP Photo/Kevin Gutting, Daily Hampshire Gazette)*

forums or social networking sites they post to or visit. In this way the physical and online places frequented by victims can be monitored to determine when they are online or nasty "ambush messages" can be left for them. Several messaging services indicate when particular users or friends are online, making it easy to pick on victims in real time.

Identifying, choosing, and targeting victims for cyberstalking is done in much the same way as in cyberbullying. The primary differences between cyberstalking and cyberbullying are the motivations involved and the usual practice of not letting on about who is stalking, which is not the case in cyberbullying because everyone tends to know who is engaged and why. Whereas bullies want their actions to become known to encourage piling on, stalkers lurk around in ways so as not to be identified. Wireless access

FALSE PERSONAL INFORMATION— PROS AND CONS

To avoid being hassled online some people do not post real information about themselves or they create fake online IDs. Many Internet users lie about their age, appearance, and other personal matters when communicating with online friends through messaging or through Web profiles—a practice that reveals the importance of *information* in online social spaces.

Online, information about identity can be falsified and played with in many ways, including modified photos, inaccurate profile information, and even false video streams. Victims as well as offenders may create false online information to avoid having their true identity known. Posting false personal information is controversial. On the one hand, deception can be used to fight online bullying and stalking by maintaining the privacy of an Internet user. Every false bit of information can lead a potential bully or stalker in the wrong direction, but it can also confuse friends and family who may not be in on the secret.

On the other hand, deception can be used to create false identities, allowing people to pretend to be someone else entirely as a means to attack others. Occasionally attackers are able to take over computer accounts in order to embarrass a victim through inappropriate actions in their name. In an incident made public by the NetSmartz Teens Web site, a girl describes how she would share all of her passwords with her best friend. One day her "friend" used one of her social networking accounts to post a modified image of the girl's face pasted onto a nude photo, quickly leading to numerous inappropriate messages from other people in her school and intense feelings of embarrassment.[4]

Similarly, false identities can be used to create the illusion that "everyone" is in on an attack. The concentrated effort of one or two people, using a series of false online identities, can give the appearance of dozens of people, all of whom are saying or doing negative things online when this is really not the situation.

to the Internet has expanded the ability of stalkers to spy on their victims.

INDIVIDUAL AND GROUP ATTACKS

Cyberbullying tends to occur in group attacks because most bullies have a need to show off and also gain support from their "toadies," followers of the bully, who are seeking their approval and eager to pile on. Sometimes groups of friends rally together to create messaging wars, but most of the time bullying involves the targeting of a single individual as a way of creating and perpetuating power.

Cyberstalking, however, tends to be committed by an individual against one or two individuals, as was the case with the Benningtons. That couple was cyberstalked for more than a year by a woman, Devon Townsend, who wanted to be closer to the band.

RAPID-FIRE, HOSTILE, AND SLY LANGUAGE

Within communication between Internet users, online incivility, foul language including racial slurs, accusations of promiscuity, abuse, and possible crime (such as threats) are common. Many Internet users believe these kinds of behavior online are to be expected and tolerated as an aspect of contemporary digital youth culture. Consequently, sending and receiving mean or nasty messages is done routinely by many Internet users. Frequently such messages are sent in the form of leetspeak, which consists of abbreviations, text symbols, and combinations of alphanumeric digits that effectively spell out words.[5] For example, a commonly used leet abbreviation is "OMG," which stands for "Oh My Gosh," or "LOL," which means "Laughing Out Loud." Less commonly used and known leet abbreviations are "POS," meaning "Parent Over Shoulder," and "PWOS," meaning "Parent Watching Over Shoulder."

Leetspeak shortens the amount of letters and words that otherwise need to be spelled out but which are difficult to type when composing with one's thumbs only on a miniature keypad. To the untrained person, leet messages can appear to be and actually become a kind of code in which the true meaning of messages is intentionally obscured or at least easily misinterpreted.[6]

ONLINE ABUSE IS OFTEN LEARNED AND IMITATED

Once someone learns how to do something, they can imitate and/or pass information along to peers. As a result, information exchanged among Internet users can quickly "go viral," meaning it spreads rapidly through social networks. Leetspeak, which is also learned and imitated, aids in rapidly disseminating information online.

An example of the spread of information is that of overcoming blocking or filtering software. Students enrolled in school-sponsored laptop programs across the country typically encounter blocked Web sites while they are learning in the classroom. However, it is common that some youth are able to find out ways around software blocking. Once this is done, the information is shared with others so that everyone can access restricted sites.

A second example includes cyberbullying. Rumors and gossip are quickly spread through social networking sites, texting, and messaging, even if the information is untrue. Messages can be delivered instantaneously and, unlike face-to-face communication, can spread to a wider population and far more quickly than via word of mouth. Thus the victims of online gossip and rumors can face serious ridicule very quickly from sizeable groups of people. Even if there is no ridicule, the victim's realization that this could occur works quickly to instill fear about what might happen if he does not get out in front of the messaging to "set the record straight," so to speak.

In some rare cases larger populations can form into highly coordinated attack groups, as message boards and wiki sites are used to post personal information about victims along with detailed bullying strategies. During such incidents entire Web pages can be taken off-line from the sheer traffic created by the number of people participating in the attack. In this type of bullying, attackers track down and publicize every piece of personal information they can find about the victim in order to expand the scope of the attack. Victims of these forms of attack nearly always report them to authorities, as anonymous bullies often call police and emergency services to the home of the victim. They also order pizzas, magazines, flowers, and other expensive services delivered to the victim's house.

LEETSPEAK AND CYBERBULLYING

Leetspeak is usually written online as "1337." The term is derived from the word *elite* to convey online stature to people skilled in using leet as a specialized form of symbolic writing. Symbols and abbreviations used in writing leet differ on various Internet forums and message boards. This means that Leet is not a universally written or understood language. Rather it exists in many different styles and dialects. According to Neel Sampat, of Rochester Institute of Technology, "Like slang terms used in other languages, leet consists of odd expressions that may have particular meaning only among certain groups of Internet users."[7] Also according to Sampat:

> Historians of Leetspeak allege that it [leet] originated within bulletin board systems (BBS) in the mid-1980s. Having elite status on a BBS allowed a user to access file folders, games, and special chat rooms, which often included archives of pirated software, pornography, or text documents documenting topics such as how to construct explosives and manufacture illicit drugs. It is also thought that leetspeak was developed to defeat text filters created by BBS or Internet Relay Chat (IRC) system operators of message boards to prevent discussion of forbidden topics such as password cracking and hacking. Originally reserved for use by hackers, crackers, and eventually the more recent generation of so-called "script kiddies," leet has entered the mainstream of MMORPGs [massively multiplayer online role-playing games] and other forms of online gaming.[8]

Leet continues to be used in online gaming and social computing forums especially to facilitate posting and receiving rapid fire messages. It is also used in cyberbullying communications and has the effect of diminishing the amount of time users have to reflect about possible consequences of particular content they are about to post. The result is that users employing leet, especially in rapid-fire situations, can become easily caught up in sending messages without pausing to think first about the possible consequences. In these situations they are also more likely to mistype messages that in turn may cloud their intentions or precise meaning of what they intend to communicate. All of this may worsen a cyberbullying conflict.

It is important to remember that the Internet never forgets. Some Internet users actually enjoy posting digital content that might include inappropriate material. Many portions of the Internet are recorded daily by private sector firms interested in tracking and data mining Internet content for commercial purposes. Some governments, including agencies of the U.S. federal government, are also known to monitor, archive, and analyze Internet content for intelligence gathering, national security, and law enforcement purposes. Millions of Internet users also save and/or repost Internet content that they find online in ad hoc manners. So even if a particular picture or video is removed from the Web by the person who originally posted it, the content may remain indefinitely. Ultimately, information—whether it be information about methods of attack, the identity of a victim, or the identity of a bully—is key in all online bullying and stalking attempts.

CONCLUSION

The process of cyberstalking and cyberbullying involves identifying, choosing, and targeting victims. This occurs as the result of perpetrators being able to establish power over victims because they are different in some way that makes them relatively easy to isolate and pick on. Individual attacks frequently expand to become group attacks through a process of piling on that occurs when friends enjoin in picking on a victim. Attacks are often carried out by using rapid-fire messaging common in contemporary digital youth culture. Sadly, foul language, including racial slurs, is commonly used in attacks. This language may aggravate matters by making messages worse in tone than basic content would otherwise convey.

Leetspeak is a technical means of abbreviating words and phrases that is used to speed up messaging in which intended meaning of things can be easily misconstrued. Leetspeak can also be used to disguise the meaning of messages, though most young and avid users of IT devices and the Internet are adept at understanding basic leet abbreviations and symbols.

4

Technologies of Cyberstalking and Cyberbullying

Alan Eisenberg is an adult blogger who now manages a Web forum for helping people prevent, overcome, and recover from bullying. On his site people relate stories about bullying. One story Eisenberg recounted on the forum was how he first experienced online bullying in the days before e-mail, social networking, IM, and cell phones. While in the fifth or sixth grade he would come home from school regularly and let himself into the house, while his parents were still at work. His friends used the phone for everything, as that was the main form of communication then. One day he answered the phone, with no parents home, and heard only heavy breathing and no answer; heavy breathing continued, and then the caller hung up. A few minutes passed and the phone rang again. More heavy breathing and then "CLICK." This pattern continued, and each time he answered only to hear breathing. Once more he answered. Again the heavy breathing started but this time the caller said in low voice, "You are dead," and then "CLICK." That was the end for that day, but the calls continued for about a week and sporadically recurred over two years.[1]

Telephones are still used to bully and the same technologies that make the Internet so easy and fun to use also create challenges for users who try to be productive and responsible when online and in off-line affairs that relate to online activities. In other words, technology is both a help and hindrance to enjoying the Net productively and responsibly. But as computerization enables users of various cultures the ability to communicate without geographic boundaries, IT devices, the Internet, and Web content also allow bullies and stalkers to track and harm their victims.

Nowadays youth and adults must understand how to protect their data, devices, information systems, and thereby themselves whenever they go online. In order to make good decisions about how to behave online, it is necessary to understand the technological ways in which cyberstalking and cyberbullying occur.

E-MAIL

E-mail is one way an online bully or cyberstalker can try to hurt his victim(s). This can involve directly sending to the victim an e-mail intended to be intimidating, harassing, threatening, or embarrassing. Once the bully is aware of the victim's e-mail address, he can send countless harassing and/or intimidating e-mails. These e-mails could contain threatening comments, including those stating that the bully plans on physically assaulting the victim or that he has a devious plan that will embarrass the victim among his peers. Even if the attacks do not happen, the victim may worry about the possibility of it for days or weeks afterward.

A variation of simply sending an abusive e-mail is to copy several other users into the distribution list, which automatically alerts a group of people to the message's contents. This tactic may well lead to piling on by others not directly involved in the actions that prompted sending the message in the first place.

Another way e-mail can be abused is by signing a victim up to receive unwanted messages or services that result in spam being sent to a victim's e-mail account. In this way victims can receive vast amounts of e-mail from potentially explicit or inappropriate content providers at his home or work e-mail. If the bully uses a school or work address, this could further distress the victim because a system administrator could view such content as inappropriate based on the acceptable use policy within the school or work environment. The result would be aggravation and embarrassment for the victim as he has tried to explain the situation to school officials, employers, or parents.

A third way that a bully may utilize e-mail to victimize a person is by forwarding e-mail messages intended for a particular individual to other people, without the sender's knowledge or permission. In this way personal information of a sensitive nature may leak out to an entire school population as each group of message recipients reads and then potentially also forwards the e-mail with or without further comment. The effect is like a snowball getting bigger and bigger as it rolls downhill but then dividing into more snowballs that repeat the process until an avalanche of what should have been private information is widespread publically.

INSTANT MESSAGING (IM)

Instant messaging provides another way for bullies to harass their victims. Ryan Halligan's suicide followed a string of IMs that included encouragement for him to kill himself. Instant messaging gives bullies numerous ways to quickly send a rude message from a computer. Rude messages can include gossip, hate speech, or profanities. Bullies can also attach pictures or other content to IMs. And as with e-mail, instant messages may be copied or forwarded to several recipients even though its contents were meant to remain private.

Another method of bullying through instant messaging includes posting mean "away messages" for anyone to see. An away message is an automated response a user sets to go to anyone who tries to send him an instant message when he is not online. Based on a person's privacy settings, an away message can be set for anyone or only certain users to read and can include any sort of message of a bullying nature. Since users (and therefore bullies) control their own account privacy settings, a mean away message once created automatically fuels more bullying anytime their account is pinged. It's like sending an IM to a friend named Sam who is not carrying his cell phone, but which automatically returns a message like, "Sam is away looking for that rat Jason!" In this case Jason has been targeted for bullying and the away message hints that others should pile on.

SMS/TEXT MESSAGING

SMS, or short message service, and text messaging amount to the same thing. When used with a cell phone, SMS-text messaging provides another rapid-fire form of messaging between peers. As with e-mail and IM, text messaging now enables inclusion of pictures and videos. This means that bullies can send extremely varied harmful text messages to any victim carrying a cell or smart phone, and like e-mail and IM, include numerous other recipients.

Mean or nasty messages sent via texting can have emotional and financial costs. Phone bills can add up depending on the terms of the users' contracts. People without unlimited text messaging may wind up with outrageous monthly bills if the cyberbullying messages are not blocked.

The advent of picture and video messaging has allowed bullies to send sexually explicit or other kinds of inappropriate images to others. Sexting has emerged as a new activity that teens and tweens take part in by sending and receiving explicit pictures and video messages of nude or partially unclothed people. Such pictures can be intended only for a boyfriend or girlfriend but can later be sent to others if a nasty breakup occurs. This in turn can be potential ammunition for bullies because the pictures can be spread quickly and instantaneously.

In May 2008, a 12-year-old girl residing in Westport, Connecticut, reportedly took a nude picture of herself during a video chat session and sent it to others online. The investigation began after word circulated in Coleytown Middle School that a nude picture was taken during a video chat among students who then shared it online. After a lengthy school and police investigation, the young girl was sent to juvenile court on "a charge of second-degree breach of peace, which involves the distribution of offensive and indecent material." Her

Technology has allowed young people to stay connected with others, but it has also increased risky behavior, including sexting and sending inappropriate or harmful images and videos. *(Source: AP Photo/Joanne Carole)*

arrest came at a time when sexting, which is illegal for minors under 18 years of age to engage in, was first becoming popular. At the time similar cases had been reported in New Jersey, New York, Alabama, Utah, Pennsylvania, and Texas.[2]

TECHNOLOGY TO COMBAT CYBERBULLYING OR CYBERSTALKING

Several different software applications are now available for purchase to help users prevent and counter cyberstalking and cyberbullying. For example, Bully Block by Parent Spy, LLC is a smart phone app that purportedly allows users to covertly record verbal threats and harassment, block inappropriate texts and pictures (e.g., sexting), and utilize auto respond features to deter offenders from leaving or sending more messages.[4] Many apps on the market can block data sent via bullies' phones along with other private and even unknown phone numbers utilized to engage in cyberbullying or cyberstalking. Some applications also feature instant reporting features that allow users to report incidents of abuse via e-mail or text messages to parents, teachers, employer human resource departments, and law enforcement. Applications may also allow incoming abusive messages (whether text or audio) along with content attached to e-mails or text messages to be stored as evidence for future inspection and downloading in support of legal actions.

In another case numerous teens in Colorado were accused of sexting in and out of school. On March 26, 2007, a prosecutor in Douglas County, Colorado, declined to prosecute 18 middle school students for exchanging nude pictures of themselves with cell phones. In that case one photo found its way onto the Internet, with very embarrassing consequences for the young people involved. In declining to prosecute, District Attorney Carol Chambers indicated that the photos were not taken in school, no group shots were taken, and no adults were involved.[3]

It is against all state and federal laws to create, possess, send, or receive photo or video content that displays the private parts of people under 18 years of age. The age of the sender does not change the law, and minors charged with sending child pornography of themselves or other underage friends are subject to prosecution. Sadly, many young people are discovering this reality the hard way. Too often such content is associated with cyberstalking and cyberbullying in ways that go beyond the control of individuals who created the content intending that it remain private. Many cyberstalkers, including child predators, seek out child pornography online and use it for all sorts of purposes. Predators have been known to blackmail youths into meeting with them in person lest a nude or compromising picture of them found online be shared with parents or authorities.

ATTACK WEB SITES AND BLOGS

Anyone can create a Web site. This has allowed young people to express their hobbies and interests, post pictures for friends and family, and post material for review by college admissions departments. Web sites can be designed using various kinds of computer code. Specific software programs are available to help people explore their interests in Web design, and these programs are useful to users who have a wide range of programming experience from beginner to advanced. Unfortunately, not everyone who creates a Web site does so with positive goals. Cyberbullies use Web sites to convey hurtful messages to targeted individuals or groups. And unlike directed or shared e-mail or IM and texting messages, Web content can be viewed by anyone with an Internet connection.

Kylie Kenney lives in Vermont. The high-tech cyberbullying that she experienced began in eighth grade and continued to her sophomore year in high school. In 2008, Kylie was standing at her locker when another student approached her and asked if she had seen a Web site about her.

At that moment Kylie had no idea what the student was talking about, but she quickly learned about an Internet site titled, "Kill Kylie Incorporated." The purpose of the Web site was to show people "how gay Kylie Kenney is..." The catch phrase was "Kylie must die." Instant messages followed with Kylie's screen name attached. Random people were sending them to other girls, including a field hockey teammate. The fabricated messages indicated that Kylie was asking these girls out on dates and included sexual advances. Extremely humiliated, Kylie filed charges with police, but could not bring back two years of her life lost over bullying, harassment, and embarrassment.[5]

Similar to Web sites, blogs also offer people the ability to share bullying content with large numbers of Internet users. Blogs are forums that allow people to post content in real time. People use blogs to post stories about their day, tips on how to do certain tasks, or other information that is important to them. This information does not need to be accurate or true and can be shared with anyone who knows the universal resource locator (URL). As such, bullies use blogs to rant or gossip about targeted victims. The amount of damage done depends in large part on how popular and widely read and responded to a blog is.

CHAT ROOMS

Chat rooms are similar to instant messaging environments but have the effect of bringing groups of people together who are interested in communicating about topics of mutual interest. Chat rooms provide larger forums of users for cyberbullies to entice or incite with bogus information. Chat room members typically engage in rapid-fire messaging. When America Online (AOL) was first available to the public, it offered its users chat rooms based on location, hobbies, health, sexuality, and other topics. Today numerous chat rooms are commonly provided by Internet Service Providers (ISPs) and Web site hosts.

Bullies can post hateful messages in chat rooms to be viewed by victims and others alike. Similar to cyberbullying content that is posted in other kinds of online forums, chat room content may leave little or no time for a victim to refute or counter untrue messages that are designed to intimidate, harass, threaten, or embarrass.

ONLINE GAMING

Online gaming is the most popular form of social computing on the Internet, with hundreds of millions of users simultaneously engaged in online play at any given time. According to Rochester Institute of Technology's Survey of Internet and At-Risk Behaviors, kindergarteners first experience online games at age four or five. So what has online gaming to do with cyberstalking and cyberbullying?

Emergence of better and more affordable computing technology has made online (and off-line electronic) gaming available to large numbers of users, including school-age children, who love to play their favorite games before or after school, on weekends, and at any other time they can access a gaming environment, perhaps even with a portable gaming device. The variety of games is extensive, and the opportunities to play games online appear endless.

Gaming bullies, also known as "griefers" or "snerts," harass fellow players in a number of ways, including "shouting" (i.e., by typing all capital letters in messages) obscenities, taunting others by name calling or putting them down, and by cheating by making up or changing rules. Griefers tend to be less interested in the game and more interested in bullying other players and disrupting online play.

Online multiplayer video games are often havens of harsh language and character abuse. Some gamers can attest to such behavior as being almost passé (i.e., occurring so often that it is hardly noticed by players who eventually come to participate and even agree with the vile language used and actions portrayed). In a word, players can become desensitized to bullying in game spaces and potentially even become bullies as they themselves compete to win.

The Internet creates the perfect storm of intense social interaction and anonymity, environments that are ripe for cyberbullying. Phrases that would be never uttered aloud in polite company find their way into microphones and online games on a regular basis.

In online gaming, players from around the world interact and socialize with each other in a game such as *Call of Duty: Black Ops*. Cyberbullies can also use online gaming as a venue to intimidate or harass others. *(Source: AP Photo/ Rich Pedroncelli)*

Such trash talk is certainly nothing new; nearly every gamer has heard it, and most gamers have probably dealt out their fair share.

Perhaps coarse language used in online gaming enclaves stems from Internet bulletin board system (BBS) history and culture in which users employed leetspeak to abbreviate and disguise their messages. Or perhaps it stems from the inherent emotional and spontaneous nature of human competition in sports or other conflicts that involve physical aggression. Not to be trivial or excuse it, but many athletes, sailors, and soldiers swear, especially when stuff happens. Kids and adults who enjoy online gaming for its intensity are apt to express and share emotional responses to success and failures. Gaming in teams also provides plenty of opportunities to rib or insult one's own team members or gamers of an opposing team.

SOCIAL NETWORKING SITES

Other kinds of social networking sites have also provided bullies a place to act and prey on their victims. Web sites such as MySpace, Facebook, and Friendster allow people the ability to post personal data, pictures, and videos. Furthermore, users can post comments onto their friend's pages if not restricted from doing so. As a result, bullies and stalkers can view a victim's page to gain information about their current activities or post humiliating and insulting images or comments.

MySpace and Facebook have received negative attention because they were among the first to produce social networking sites accessed primarily by unsupervised young people. In January 2008, in response to concerns about the online safety of youth who used its forums, MySpace agreed to work with 49 state attorneys general offices and the District of Columbia to establish a "set of principles to combat harmful material on social-networking sites (pornography, harassment, cyberbullying, and identity theft, among other issues), better educate parents and schools about online threats, cooperate with law enforcement officials around the country, as well as develop new technology for age and identity verification on social-networking sites."[6]

Hundreds of other social networking companies with Web page offerings similar to those provided by MySpace and Facebook also exist in what remains a largely unregulated industry. Consequently, although improvements in the monitoring of mean-spirited messages have increased, too many cyberbullying comments are made every day for system administrators to monitor them all. The result is that when users go online, they must be prepared for the possibility of being flamed (i.e., insulted in some way).

Social networking sites are the main tools through which people make friends online and maintain relationships with friends, family members, and coworkers. Too often, however, these sites are places in which relationships can take a turn for the worst. Boyfriends and girlfriends may post or send nasty messages during a fight or breakup. Also, cyberbullies and cyberstalkers can use social networking site features such as wall boards to gain information about potential victims, post abusive comments, or spy on their victims to monitor their reactions once online attacks are made.

ANONYMOUS IMAGE BOARDS AND WIKIS

Anonymous image boards and wiki sites have become common tools in extremely large and distributed bullying attacks. Both are Web tools that allow users to create and edit messages while linking to other Web content. They enable users to post images without necessarily providing personal or verifiable information about themselves. Sites are set up to allow this and administrators typically pledge to delete or otherwise not to reveal Internet service provider (ISP) information to authorities. Anonymous image boards first appeared in Japan as a way to allow anime and video game fans to quickly and easily post images and have conversations. Today these boards are sometimes used by pedophiles and child pornographers to view and post images of naked children or underage teens posing in sexually suggestive ways. Since anonymous boards and wikis are not frequently used for productive purposes they have gained a certain level of notoriety as the "toilets" of the Internet, often filled with graphic images, vulgar humor, and hateful messages.

Occasionally, people will become targeted by the users of such sites, most frequently because they themselves have engaged in some form of highly visible inappropriate activity online that has "gone viral." Attacks usually start once someone posts some initial information about the victim onto one of the many anonymous image boards. Other users then begin to track personal information—including phone number, home address, school, and place of work—in order to attack the victim.

CALLER ID, GPS, AND CALL VIDEO TECHNOLOGY

Caller ID, GPS (global positioning system), and call-video-enabled cell phones may also be changing the technological playing field for bullies and stalkers and their victims. Caller ID

RETALIATION BULLYING— IS IT EVER JUSTIFIED?

Anonymous image and wiki sites often keep posts online for a very short period of time. So they are commonly used to host information about targets in a central location. In one of the most publicized incidents, two masked teenage boys posted a video onto YouTube in which they repeatedly abused a cat. They were quickly identified and targeted by anonymous image board users. Although YouTube took the videos down, attackers had made copies, and they used small details in the videos to eventually find the teenagers. Once they were identified, thousands of messages and phone calls were sent to the teens and to their parents, their school, local law enforcement, and local and national media outlets. This story made local and regional news, and the teens were eventually brought to trial for their actions. Many of the Web sites brought online simply to publicize the story and spread the personal information of the boys still remain online today. While this particular example may seem a justified use of Internet bullying, not all such incidents involving anonymous image boards have been so seemingly well meaning.

makes it possible for victims (and offenders) to see who is calling before choosing to answer an incoming phone call. This can be advantageous if someone suspects a bully or stalker may be calling and wishes not to speak to them. However, bullies and stalkers can also use caller ID to discern whether messages they have left are beginning to have effects either on victims targeted for abuse or, in cases of cyberbullying, on other people incited to pile on. Suppose a victim sets her phone to block receiving future calls from a bully, or changes her voice mail to express a "To hell with you guys!" message—both indicate the victim is becoming rattled and that additional bullying tactics are needed. Deletions in personal profile content or more restrictive privacy settings can also signal to a cyberbully or stalker that he is getting to his victim. Bullies and stalkers can also use "friend finder" apps to locate potential victims to target. These tools, along with powerful Web browsers, enable abusers to rather easily locate updated personal information about nearly anyone with an online presence or profile. All technology is subject to being abused as it evolves and becomes increasingly integrated into commercial products. GPS technology potentially adds a future dimension to bullying and cyberstalking because satellites can nearly pinpoint where calls are made from or received. With the location information of calls placed or received, victims and bullies or stalkers could potentially plot their next moves, literally, as they move from one place to another. In April 2011, it was revealed that iPhones transmitted GPS locations of Wi-Fi hotspot locations from where messages are sent or received. This revelation caused quite a stir among users and privacy advocates. Apple responded to explain that iPhones are programmed to store location information to expedite data processing when customers use mapping and route-finding tools that come installed on the device. An Apple representative reportedly said that, "Calculating a phone's location using just GPS satellite data can take up to several minutes. iPhone can reduce this time to just a few seconds by using Wi-Fi hotspot and cell tower data to quickly find GPS satellites, and even triangulate its location using just Wi-Fi hotspot and cell tower data when GPS is not available (such as indoors or in basements)."[7] The firm also assured users that Apple does not centrally track users. However, location data is stored on a local file which, when analyzed using an OS X app, can reportedly reveal where a user was when sending or receiving data.[8]

Technology that would allow ordinary users, including cyberbullies or stalkers, to access GPS data of users in real time is not currently available for purchase. Nonetheless the future possibility of tracking people in real time while they are using mobile IT devices is important because so much off-line bullying involves physical face-to-face contact, while stalking can also involve physical spying if offenders follow their victims around. Currently certain cars have GPS tracking capabilities that enable savvy bullies and stalkers to locate their victims while victims are driving or riding in a car so equipped. Conceivably victims could also benefit from such technology that allows them to locate bullies and stalkers, although offenders are more likely to deactivate GPS features or devices to avoid being tracked.

Call video technology provides a third way in which bullying and stalking may be changing. Cell phones with cameras that are programmed to broadcast the user's facial images and expressions when she is on a call can allow offenders to see their victims' emotional reactions. It is possible that video calling technology could work in reverse by allowing victims to see bullies or stalkers when they call, but it is likely a bully or stalker would disable this feature.

CONCLUSION

Nearly every form of Internet communication available can be used for cyberstalking and cyberbullying. This should come as no surprise because these kinds of abuse are about communicating through written or spoken words often combined with visual images such as still photos or videos. Internet technologies assist bullies by allowing them to spread their negative messages and avoid detection. Internet technologies also assist stalkers by allowing them to gather information about possible victims to aid in choosing particular people to target.

Cyberbullies and cyberstalkers can use many technological methods to carry out attacks on victims. E-mail, instant messaging (IM), text messaging, attacks via Web sites and blogs, chat rooms, online gaming forums, social networking sites, anonymous image boards, and wikis are all technical means through which one may harass, intimidate, embarrass, or threaten another person. GPS technology may conceivably also be used alone or in combination with the technologies listed here for purposes of cyberbullying or cyber-stalking. Being familiar with Internet methods and technologies can go a long ways toward avoiding trouble online.

It is possible that Internet technologies can also be used to protect Internet users from stalking and bullying. This is demonstrated by the tactic of creating false information or using devices and features such as caller ID, and possibly even GPS and video calling to learn more about, dissuade, or avoid cyberstalking and cyberbullying.

What Is It Like to Be Bullied or Stalked Online?

In 2005, the New Hampshire Crimes Against Children Research Center (CCRC) published the results of a major study on youth Internet safety, in which they interviewed hundreds of students about their experiences online. Many described what it was like to be stalked or bullied online:[1]

- *Girl, 12 years old: "These people from school were calling me a prostitute and whore...and saying I was raped. [The bullying happened] because I'm an easy target. I didn't let it bother me until about a month ago and [then] I started getting physical with people."*
- *Boy, 10 years old: "This person, she gave me her address and told me to come over. I said no, and then she started typing in bad words. There are a lot of people out there that do a lot of stuff...I think they were trying to make me come over there to kidnap me."*

- *Boy, 12 years old:* "I was at my cousin's house on his computer, and we were playing games. A pop-up came up, and it said, 'I know where you live,' and it showed a map of the area we lived in. It scared me."
- *Boy, 14 years old:* "I have my own…Web site, and I have my own page on it, and someone posted something bad about me on it."
- *Boy, 15 years old:* "My cousin had my password and went into…a blog…and pretended to be me and wrote that I [laugh] liked to smell people. He put it in my…profile too. [It happened] because I did it to him."
- *Girl, 16 years old:* "Someone that I go to school with started spreading rumors about me by posting things in chat rooms and sending e-mails that were talking about me doing sexual things with all these different guys that were not true at all. I didn't even know the guys. [It happened] because at one point I got mad, and we had a confrontation. [She was] doing these things to get back at me—for revenge."

At some point in their lives nearly everyone has experienced the strange feeling of being watched or followed. Perhaps it was in a local shopping mall, with a sense of being watched from behind by someone sneaking around or lurking from places unseen. Or perhaps it was while walking down a street after dark or while in a wooded park that cast shadows from trees. The sound of footsteps creaking on boards, a person's scream, an animal's howl, or even breaking glass can all send tingles up a person's spine in the right circumstances.

Stalking and long-term bullying can also feel like this, except that the experience is repeated over and over, slowly wearing down a victim over a period of time. Even online, in the absence of dark, lonely places and creaking floorboards, a victim can feel dread as the instant message chimes with what could be another intimidating message from an offender. Or perhaps it could be a feeling of suspicion about every online friend request as in cases in which an offender pretends to be someone else in order to get close to a victim.

The simple fact is that bullying and stalking are societal problems that have always existed in various forms. The Internet and widespread use of IT devices has created more ways for these abusive behaviors to occur while increasing potential harm experienced by affected individuals, families, and groups of people within society. Whether computing technology is involved or not, being bullied or stalked can be horrific.

FEAR, MENTAL DISTRESS, AND PSYCHOLOGICAL HARM

Bullies and stalkers find many ways to manipulate people and make them feel sad, angry, and scared. Victims of cyberstalking and cyberbullying in turn experience considerable amounts of fear, mental distress, and psychological harm. These effects worsen over time if attacks are not stopped. In addition, impacts of bullying and stalking cannot be easily reversed. Once started, gossip spreads, and so does the damage it causes to victims.

Similarly, personal or sensitive information or photographs once distributed online may become viral and not be retrievable. Even if intimidating, harassing, threatening, or embarrassing content could be taken off-line before spreading, it cannot also be erased from the minds of people who read or saw it. Indeed, constant thoughts of the bully's actions remain at the front and center of a victim's mind. As a result, the victim experiences fear of re-victimization day after day, sometimes for weeks or months. In chronic instances coping with the impact may require professional counseling, psychiatric treatment, or other medical services.

According to research, young people reported being upset, frightened, or embarrassed about half of the time as a result of bullying or stalking. One out or three victims reported symptoms of stress following cyberbullying or cyberstalking, causing many to stay off the Internet. Some victims also reported an inability to stop thinking about the online bullying or stalking, or a feeling

Bullying can cause victims to feel sad, angry, and depressed. Targets of cyberbullying often withdraw from the Internet and feel stressed or anxious. *(Source: © John Birdsall/The Image Works)*

of nervousness or jumpiness. Among adult victims of stalking, 46 percent felt stressed by not knowing what a perpetrator would do next, and 29 percent were afraid or felt abusive behavior would never stop.[2]

DISTRUST, LOST FRIENDSHIPS, AND SOCIAL ISOLATION

Feeling sad, angry, embarrassed, hurt, or scared is common and perfectly normal among victims of cyberstalking and cyberbullying. In fact, most victims of bullying feel a combination of those feelings and over time can feel different ways about attacks they experience and the people responsible. With instilled fear that a victim may be attacked again, it is common for victims to lose trust in people to whom they are close. Frequently they become unsure of whom to trust and become increasingly disinclined to share personal information so as to feel less vulnerable and more protected.

Losing trust in one's friends invariably breaks down friendships and can lead to a victim's self-imposed social isolation. Of course, bullies and those who pile on to worsen bullying often shun victims in order to make them feel even more isolated as part of their bullying. Over time as victims lose faith in current relationships they may lose confidence in their ability to make new friends. All this reinforces social isolation that causes victims to feel so very alone much of the time.

Social isolation typically results in victims withdrawing from sports or club activities and finding more things to do alone. School work can also suffer as victims feel like they cannot work comfortably with other students. If not addressed, depression and thoughts of suicide can creep into victims' minds as they wrestle with feelings of sadness, anger, and giving up on so many things they once cared for.

Some cases become so severe that the victim needs to seek counseling or other professional mental health assistance to help manage depression. Left untreated, mentally unhealthy victims may experience even more dangerous health problems. The most severe cases involve eating disorders and even self-mutilation that result from victims feeling the need to punish themselves for being overweight or not sufficiently thin.

PROPERTY DAMAGE AND PHYSICAL HARM

Though it happens less often than mental trauma, victims of cyberstalking and cyberbullying may also experience property damage and physical harm to their bodies. As they do in face-to-face interactions, cyberbullies and cyberstalkers can also inflict physical harm and cause property damage online via hardware hacking, password cracking, sending e-mail and IM spam, or distributing malware (i.e., malicious computer code such as viruses, Trojans, worms, or spyware). In a physical interaction between a bully and a victim, a bully can push or punch a victim, causing the victim undue pain. Cyberbullies can attack a victim's hard drive, home, or even physically harm the victim by contact after the online interaction. Such harm can occur in both public and private places.

FINANCIAL COSTS AND EXPENSES

Severe financial burdens can be placed on victims after they have been bullied or stalked. Although rarely affecting children directly, parents and adults must often endure financial costs associated with damage to property, workplaces, and homes, plus expenses associated with physical and mental well-being, such as counseling and medical treatment. Some costs pertain to protecting oneself while attacks are ongoing. Once attacked, a victim is constantly on the defense and worried about potential future attacks and expenses. For example, depending on the psychological state and circumstances of a teenage victim, one or both parents may have to take time off from work to attend counseling appointments, court proceedings, and, in worst-case scenarios, potentially face the decision of quitting their job, resulting in complete loss of income. Lack of money to pay for monthly bills and take care of family members places increased stress on the victim. Additional long-term costs may be incurred after attacks end as victims struggle to put their lives back in order.

BULLYING INVOLVING PROPERTY DAMAGE

In 2007, Paul was a new middle school student who became enrolled midyear after the holiday season when his family moved from Michigan to Minnesota. Other students immediately began to check him out because he was a new kid in school. Instantly the basis for new friendships was created, but so too were ill feelings about Paul being an exceptionally gifted athlete, as became obvious during gym class. After the first day of school, as Paul prepared to go home, he went to the bike rack only to find an ice pick stuck in one tire of his bicycle. Attached to the ice pick was a note that read, "Hey superstar, try being an athlete now!"

Fixing Property Damages

One form of damage a victim may incur as the result of cyberbullying is having to repair or replace property damages. For instance, a bully could send a computer virus to the victim's computer, which could cause the victim's hard drive to crash if it is not properly protected. This can be quite damaging to the victim, especially if she has no backup options, is unable to recover lost data, or cannot afford to buy a new computer.

Another example of damage could stem from a cyberbully teasing a victim online and then causing physical harm and/or property damage at a public place such as a school or workplace. A bully might tamper with or damage his victim's personal property or merely threaten to do so. It is also possible for a bully to threaten via instant messaging to harm a victim's car at school. While the victim may feel unsafe and worried about taking his car to school, he may have no other option. Thus the bully could "key" the car, puncture the tires, or cause even greater damage.

Medical Expense Due to Injuries or Emotional Trauma

Cyberbullying or cyberstalking can cause stress, trauma, and mental harm. When psychological harm rises to a level requiring professional treatment in the form of counseling, prescription drugs, or visits to emergency rooms, financial costs can quickly soar to hundreds and even thousands of dollars. Poor and disabled people may need to rely on the federal government's Medicaid program to help cover such costs. Even if a victim has private medical insurance to offset costs, *someone* ends up paying for costs of treatment. Indirect costs paid by Medicaid or otherwise borne by society as a whole are referred to as tertiary costs. Just as shoplifting costs society more money as prices of store items are raised to cover theft, cyberstalking and cyberbullying indirectly raise costs of medical programs or insurance that everyone in society pays for either in taxes or insurance premiums.

Relocation to New School, Neighborhood, and/or Workplace

A person who is victimized by a bully or stalker faces emotional distress that can hinder progress in their school or workplace. In school, children must face their attacker. Children do not want to be humiliated or teased by bullies in front of their classmates. In bad cases it is best for a child to relocate to a new school (or community) so she can have a new start among people who are not familiar with her past. A home should be a place of comfort and peace, a refuge for those that have been bullied or stalked, but it can also inspire awful memories of bullying that occurred there. As a result, in severe cases of bullying or stalking, people may choose to move to a new house to avoid further harassment and bad memories. When they do so, large moving expenses are incurred. Moving, or other circumstances, such as a bully being a coworker, may also require victims to quit their job and find new employment to escape the bully.

Lawsuits and Costs to the Judicial System

Victims of any form of crime may be required to attend court sessions to help prosecute the offender. To do so, victims must take time off from work or school. As a result, victims must ask their employers or school administrators for time off. Not only can this cost victims lost wages or put them behind on schoolwork, but it can also cause further psychological trauma if the victim must revisit the attacker's actions when examined in the court room or when explaining why they must be excused from work or school.

In order for victims to receive justice, many victims feel that they must seek legal action against their attacker either through criminal prosecution, a civil law suit, or both. Numerous cases of cyberstalking and cyberbullying have been heard in civil and criminal court. With any court case, however, the victim may incur costs in order to pay for transportation to and from the courtroom, and may also lose wages. Sometimes in criminal cases a judge can order a convicted person (or the parents) to pay fines to compensate victims for property damages or other expenses. This is rare, which is why victims (or their parents, in cases involving minors) sue bullies or stalkers (or their parents) in addition to seeking criminal prosecution. If they do elect to sue, they may also incur legal expenses in order to hire lawyers to represent them and/or their child.

In a case in Kansas City, Kansas, a jury awarded Dylan Theno $250,000 against the Tonganoxie School District for years of bullying due to the false rumor that he was gay.[3] Even with such an award, a large portion of the money often goes to pay attorney and court-related costs. Furthermore, the psychological harm will not likely be offset with a financial disbursement offered by the defense once an offender is convicted. Moreover, sanctions imposed on offenders by judges in criminal and civil cases that center on bullying or stalking are known to vary widely, though systematic study of these variances is not known to exist.

Circumstances including the nature and extent of harms experienced by victims can vary substantially. Obviously a wrongful death case is far more serious than one involving only property damage. In general, victims in relatively serious versus minor cases, whether of a criminal or civil nature, can expect respectively harsher sentences and larger financial judgments to be imposed against offenders. But sanctions such as jail time, fines, community service, probation, and civil awards vary widely to reflect the amount of harm and other case circumstances involved. A victim who experiences physical injury, psychological harm, and property damage is likely to be compensated more than a person whose reputation was temporarily trashed on a Web site. Similarly, first-time offenders usually receive lighter sentences than repeat offenders. In determining sanctions to impose, judges consider case circumstances carefully. In trying to be consistent and fair, they may also consider sanctions imposed by judges (or

RESTORATIVE JUSTICE: AN ALTERNATIVE TO CRIMINAL AND CIVIL COURT CASES

Karl, a sophomore in high school at Forest Hill Community School in England, was known to terrorize other boys, particularly a boy named Jerry (the same age). Threats made in school and outside of school scared Jerry so much that he was afraid to attend school. He even spent his holiday break locked in his own home because Karl lived in the same neighborhood. Teachers would punish Karl at school, but the bullying did not stop. Jerry's teachers thought that the problem was handled, but oftentimes the bullying continued the next day.

Despite this history of bullying, Jerry and Karl are now friends and get along harmoniously. Karl has stopped bullying Jerry, who has gained some confidence and is becoming more involved in school. Why the change? Restorative justice had been implemented into the school as a supplement and possible alternative to traditional criminal prosecution and civil case law suits. Rather than imposing traditional sanctions for harms caused, restorative justice seeks community harmony and forgiveness through understanding and reconciliation between offenders and victims.

juries) in previous similar cases within the same or a different court jurisdiction. Even so, sanctions will vary greatly, sometimes even in similar cases. Not everyone will be satisfied with the outcome of their case—a sense of justice having not been served is periodically felt by victims despite a judge's best efforts to be fair to everyone involved.

CONCLUSION

Feeling sad or threatened by a bully or stalker can affect a victim in a variety of ways. Fear, mental distress, and psychological

Forest Hill Community School has been using restorative justice for several years, and was one of the first in the United Kingdom to do so. All other area schools, as well as the Youth Offending Team and school resource officers, were offered restorative justice training. In this case Deputy Mike Levens used restorative justice to bring the two boys face to face with one another. Jerry was asked to explain what had been the worst thing about Karl's mistreatment. Karl was appalled by what he heard. He said, "I thought I'd just been pushing him about, telling him to get out my face, but really I was making the boy frightened. He didn't even want to leave his house all Christmas. I felt awful. After that I thought, I can't do this no more."

Karl was not negatively punished for his actions, rather he listened to Jerry explain how the bullying affected him. Jerry was relieved Karl wasn't suspended for bullying him. "I don't think him not coming to school would have been an answer—it was better to work it out there and then go through the whole thing of you being scared when he comes back," Jerry said. Punishment only ends in more anger. As for the parents, they often need time to appreciate the benefits of restorative justice. Perhaps in the end most victims and their parents, especially in cases not involving significant lasting harms, can be satisfied with an apology along with assurances the bullying will stop.[4]

harm, as well as distrustfulness and lost friendships are common. In advanced cases of cyberstalking and cyberbullying victims can become socially isolated from their friends and peers, alone in their thoughts, frustrations, and anger. Since so much about bullying goes unreported or is not taken seriously when reported, victims may experience feelings of being alone within themselves, which can lead to even worse emotional or psychological trauma. Recovering from this trauma may even require professional counseling or other forms of treatment. Other potential consequences of cyberstalking and cyberbullying include property damage and also physical harm ranging from minor to very serious injuries that require emergency or other medical treatment.

Consequences of victimization often involve financial costs associated with fixing broken property, paying medical expenses, and even paying relocation costs of moving to a new home, school district, or job. Lawsuits and costs to juvenile and adult justice systems can also involve large sums of money. In some sense, everyone in society pays for the costs of cyberstalking and cyberbullying.

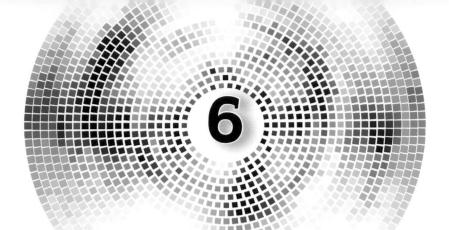

What Authorities Are Doing to Stop Cyberstalking and Cyberbullying

On October 17, 2006, a 13-year-old girl named Megan Meier, who lived in Dardenne Prairie, Missouri, committed suicide allegedly due to cyberbullying. Megan, like many other young people, had joined MySpace. Within a short period of time she was called a whore and a liar. Megan "friended" a 16-year-old boy named Josh Evans who left her comments of flattery and friendliness. After a month, however, his nice comments turned into harmful and threatening messages, including, "I hate you." Megan, who suffered from depression, hung herself in her bedroom using a belt soon after this. The last message Megan sent to Josh stated, "I just don't understand why u acttin like this."[1] Investigators found out that the profile of Josh Evans was in fact created by a 19-year-old woman, Ashley Grills, and a 48-year-old woman named Lori Drew who lived in the same neighborhood. Drew had created the profile to monitor Megan's comments to her daughter.

At the time of Megan's death prosecutors were unable to bring charges against the two under Missouri state criminal law, which did not prohibit cyberbullying. Nearly two years later, however, on May 15, 2008, Lori Drew was indicted by a federal grand jury on three counts of illegally accessing an Interstate (Internet) computer system to inflict emotional distress, and one count of conspiracy for plotting with another person to harm Megan. This case, which received national attention, inspired the Megan Meier Cyberbullying Prevention Act of 2009, the first national legislation to propose banning cyberbullying. This federal law was not enacted by Congress, but the Megan Meier case and other tragic cyberbullying cases, some involving suicides, inspired Missouri and numerous other states to pass anti-cyberbullying crime laws. In 2011, 49 states had enacted such laws.

Bullying and stalking are societal problems that have always existed in various forms. The Internet and widespread use of IT devices has created more ways for these to occur while increasing potential harm experienced by individuals, families, and groups within society. Various groups are responsible for preventing and controlling cyberstalking and cyberbullying, but the unfortunate realities of bullying and stalking and the constraints on what can be done to stop or deter them mean law enforcement, school officials, and parents face a struggle to protect youth online.

ONLINE ABUSE AND THE LAW

There are now many legal ramifications for cyberstalking and cyberbullying. Legislatures are now enacting laws to punish cyberbullies and stalkers. According to Rhode Island Senator John Tassoni, who introduced a bill in 2007 to study cyberbullying, "The kids are forcing our hands to do something legislatively."[2] Many people believe, however, that such legislation would be ineffective. George McDonough, an education coordinator with the Rhode Island Department of Education, believes that the Internet has become an "instant slam book."[3] As a result, he believes the best way to solve the problem of cyberstalking and cyberbullying is by teaching social norms that include how to be respectful online instead of legislating against disrespectful communications.

Laws are not always followed, and it is necessary to teach children and adults the importance of cyberethics and respect online. With the rise of any form of crime, resources exist within judicial systems to handle cases that must be heard. Law enforcement teams must be trained to handle such cases and social workers must be present to help victims of cyberstalking and cyberbullying. In addition, with an increase of cyberbullying cases, judges must be available as well as other courtroom personnel. Furthermore, detention centers must have the capacity to house an increase in criminals who are prosecuted and convicted in court. All members of the judicial system are affected by an increase in cyberstalking and cyberbullying cases. This situation is worsened as officials struggle to address new forms of cyberstalking and cyberbullying made possible by technology.

Recall that in the cyberbullying case involving the death of Megan Meier, Missouri prosecutors were unable to apply existing state laws to bring charges against Lori Drew, who was found through investigation to have created a false MySpace account. Drew allegedly accomplished this from her home computer in Missouri via MySpace servers located in California. In 2008, approximately two years after Missouri prosecutors declined to prosecute Drew on existing state charges, she was indicted by federal authorities under provisions of the 1986 Computer Fraud and Abuse Act. Prosecutors applied this law in conjunction with provisions of the Interstate Commerce Clause of the U.S. Constitution. Although initially convicted by a federal jury of three misdemeanor charges, Drew later received a direct acquittal from presiding federal judge George Wu, who believed the government had overreached in attempting to prosecute her.[4]

The use of information technologies for abusive behavior had been a problem long before the problems with Lori Drew and Megan Meier, as should be no surprise. In fact, cyberbullying and similar

Lori Drew (with daughter Sarah) was brought up on fraud charges, in con-nection to the death of teenager Megan Meier. Drew was one of the people involved in using the online social network MySpace to harass Meier, who committed suicide. *(Source: AP Photo/Nick Ut)*

types of issues have been in and out of the courts since at least 1995. A case that year concerned a senior honor student at Newport High School in Bellevue, Washington, who had developed a Web page detailing the purported sex lives of his friends on the football team. As punishment, school administrators recalled all of the recom-mendation letters that had been sent to college admissions board on behalf of the student and additionally revoked his National Merit Scholarship. However, in this early case, it was the creator of the offensive Web page, rather than any of the potential "victims," who instigated the court case. The student claimed that the school had violated his free speech rights when they forced him to take the site down, and punished him for its creation. Ultimately the case was settled out of court, but it highlighted issues with freedom of speech

SHOULD STATES STANDARDIZE CYBER-BULLYING LAWS AND PENALTIES?[5]

During September 2010, " . . . at least nine American teen-agers killed themselves as a direct result of bullying and intimidation by their peers. In all but one of those cases, boys and girls were harassed, assaulted, and slandered because of their sexuality. The youngest was only 11 years old. The Internet, especially social networks, played a role in every case: Rumors spread via malicious texts, and threats routinely appeared on victims' Facebook pages and Twitter accounts. In the most outrageous and widely publicized case, antagonists surreptitiously webcast a sexual encounter between a male Rutgers University undergraduate and another man. Publicly humiliated, Tyler Clementi, one of the men in the webcast, leaped to his death from the George Washington Bridge."

Following this series of youth suicides, serious debate ensued about whether to consistently criminalize or decriminalize bullying across states that historically have maintained similar, though differing, juvenile justice system laws, procedures and penalties. Forty-one American states have anti-bullying laws, but the country has no single standard or definition, and none of the laws specifically address issues of Internet attacks. Many child advocates, ironically, oppose criminalizing bullying, because they fear the long-term consequences of saddling juveniles with criminal records. More importantly, they stress criminal punishment of a few offenders does not serve as warning for other bullies, because the adolescent mindset includes the idea "that never will happen to me."

Brooke Sommerfield, a Southern California child advocate, suggests, "Civil litigation represents the best option for victims and their families, because every bullying incident is, almost by definition, a case of personal injury. I believe we should hold parents accountable for their children's behaviour, and I think we should hold schools accountable for their negligence. A few hefty 'wrongful death' awards will send the strong message the community needs to hear." Sommerfield emphasizes that every act generally regarded as bullying already is recognized as a "tort" in civil law, and therefore gives victims and families grounds for filing suit.[6]

online and the ability of schools to punish students for activities that took place out of school.

In the time between the Newport High School case and the Megan Meier case, various similar cases were brought to court, often with similar results, including dismissal of charges and pretrial out-of-court settlements. For criminal cyberbullying cases that go to court, in which the offender is charged with violation of criminal law, as in the Drew and Meier case, prosecutors have historically struggled to stretch existing laws to fit the circumstances. New state-level anti-cyberbullying laws may change the outcome of future criminal cases, or not, depending on how trial and appellate court judges rule on their constitutionality. Heretofore, civil cyberbullying cases have involved bullying victims and offenders as plaintiffs. Both types of cases have been won and lost. Cases in which offenders sue school districts or employers for violating free speech rights, as with the Newport case, generally have come out in favor of the plaintiff, meaning the accused bully.

These are major reasons that have slowed the development and testing of cyberstalking and cyberbullying laws. On the one hand, lawmakers see a need for anti-bullying legislation, but on the other hand, constitutional free speech rights must be very carefully protected. It would be unreasonable for lawmakers to propose a cyberbullying law that said, "You have the right to freedom of speech, unless you're being mean."

WHAT DO POLICE DO? WHAT CAN THEY DO?

On October 15, 2010, officers of the King County Sheriff's Department near Seattle, Washington, arrested William Pritchard, 23, for cyberstalking. Allegedly in a three-month period of time, Pritchard sent 269 voice or e-mails to a 17-year-old girl he was stalking on MySpace. In the process he threatened to kill the girl along with her entire family and also carve his name onto her chest if she did not send him nude photos of herself. Threats continued for several months before law enforcement was notified and became involved.[7] Prosecutors alleged numerous counts

In 2008, Idaho launched a statewide Internet Crimes Against Children Task Force to help protect young people from cyberbullying, cyberstalking, and other online crimes. *(Source: AP Photo, Idaho Press-Tribune, Mike Vogt)*

of cyberstalking, communicating with a minor for immoral purposes, harassment, and extortion. A twice-convicted cyberstalker, Pritchard was sentenced in March 2011, to five and a half years for his actions in this case.[8]

While cyberstalking may be a relatively new type of crime, the police are equipped to handle such cases. Police are trained professionals ready to serve and protect the community. Police respond to various incidents such as car accidents, robberies, and shootings. Officers also walk and drive around communities to monitor neighborhoods. It is important for citizens to feel safe around police officers to create a sense of security.

Everyday computing technology has also helped many police departments in their daily activities. For example, police use GPS technology to monitor their police cars and help officers find a distressed person's location. Police also use cell phone technology to stay in touch with each other. Police agencies across the country are now updating their computer equipment to investigate cases of computer crime and abuse. Agencies are also hiring investigators who have IT knowledge as well as a criminal justice background. Computer forensics is an important part of solving cases of cyberstalking and cyberbullying. An investigator may search an offender's hard drive for incriminating text or pictures or even subpoena the Internet service provider for a user's Internet logs.

In cases of cyberstalking and cyberbullying it is important for victims and bystanders to feel confident and comfortable in talking with the police. Once someone has been bullied or stalked, it is crucial for her to report such behavior to a trusted adult such as a parent, teacher, or police officer. Once the police hear the story, they can then take appropriate steps toward protecting the victim from future attacks. In general, police can further assist victims by being responsive, attentive, compassionate, encouraging, supportive, and expert in what they do. When police officers do not act professionally, or do not take cyberbullying or cyberstalking seriously, victims lose confidence in law enforcement officers, believing they do not care and/or are incapable of helping them. If this happens often, entire communities may lose confidence in their local law enforcement agencies if not in the entire criminal justice system.

Law enforcement agencies are increasingly joining forces with the community to stay current about cyberthreats and trends, and related safety issues and laws. They must continue to become knowledgeable about technology, social networking sites and digital youth culture, along with harmful aspects of ways in which some youth behave online. In appropriate ways and extents, law enforcement must assimilate into teen online culture to learn why youth behave as they do and to get a better sense of how serious online messages that incorporate leetspeak or coarse language may actually be. Collaborating with parents, students, and educators in the process is important. For example, Colorado Springs Detective Rick Hunt promotes a video on cybersafety that his agency created.[9] It includes helpful hints and steps that parents can use to prevent cyberthreats and figure out if their child is being bullied. Police also periodically engage in public awareness campaigns, sometimes in partnership with nonprofit organizations, to promote cybersafety.

In 1998, the Department of Justice began to provide funding for the establishment of state and local Internet Crimes Against Children (ICAC) task forces. While these task forces were not originally established to fight the contemporary issues of cyberstalking and cyberbullying—which were much smaller problems at the time—the training they provide gives law enforcement officers the knowledge and skills necessary to act against online crimes against children, while collaborating with other similar task forces across state lines. Task forces are created in an attempt to deal with the jurisdiction problems that exist when Internet-based abuses occur across geographic boundaries like county or state lines. Originally, task forces primarily handled issues of child pornography and online sex predation, but they have since branched out to include bullying and stalking investigations. Today law enforcement officers are eager to investigate any cases of online abuse that involve children. Officers have also begun to take on the responsibility of educating schools, parents, and communities on Internet safety issues.

THE ROLE OF SCHOOL OFFICIALS AND TEACHERS

School officials and teachers play an important role in preventing cyberstalking and cyberbullying. A 2002 study involving 196 ninth-grade students showed that only 35 percent believed their teachers were interested in stopping bullying, as opposed to only 25 percent who believed administrators were interested in stopping bullying.[10] Furthermore, the 2006 Fight Crime study conducted by Opinion Research Corporation shows that only 9 percent of 12- to 17-year-olds who had been cyberbullied told a teacher about it.[11] As a result, one of the first problems school officials and teachers face includes the lack of accurate reporting of cyberbullying and stalking cases by youth. How can teachers and administrators respond to cyberbullying and stalking incidents if they are unaware of the problem?

Furthermore, if students feel like they are not being adequately supervised and guided in responsible online activities, they will not feel compelled to talk to teachers about their problems.

Another concern faced by school officials and teachers is the lack of education and training among teachers regarding how to protect and help students involved in cyberbullying and stalking cases. Teacher development courses need to be offered so that teachers can feel confident in assisting in situations involving cyberbullying and

CYBERSAFETY EDUCATION KIDS NEED IN SCHOOL

In general, people of all ages need more knowledge and skills in how to remain safe, secure, and responsible when using the Internet. Education received by students in all grades must be relevant and age-appropriate in its delivery method and content. Ideally youth safety education should also be interesting and enjoyable for students. This should not be too difficult to achieve given the natural curiosity and love of IT devices that kids have, especially when it comes to electronic gaming, and the inherent richness of Internet content.

Several Web-based learning programs have already been developed. I-SAFE, developed by i-SAFE, Inc. of Carlsbad, California, and NetSmartz, developed by the National Center for Missing and Exploited Children (NCMEC) located in Washington, D.C., are two such programs. Each has been preliminarily evaluated in its ability to provide for student learning, knowledge retention, and changing ways in which students think about and use the Internet. Both programs have online learning modules for students of different ages, and for teachers and parents. Learning modules cover cyberstalking and cyberbullying among many other topics. Modules for middle and high school students feature peer instruction in which students in seventh through twelfth grades provide instruction in ways youth readily identify with.

stalking. It is also important for school administrators and teachers to be aware of their students' personal lives. By doing so, they can monitor emotional distress inflicted by bullies and stalkers.

In 2011, faculty of the Rochester Institute of Technology, with funding support from the Internet Safety Coalition (IKeepSafe) and on behalf of the U.S. Department of Justice, provided professional development for teachers, IT professionals, and administrators working in New York State elementary schools. The training was

Development of sound cybersafety, security, and ethics educa-tion has been a long time in coming and is still being improved. Throughout the years, as parents, educators, and law enforcement officers recognized Internet dangers, especially those related to online sexual predation, ad hoc presentations usually given by police officers were provided in schools. Often these presentations employed scare tactics that overemphasized the dangers of sexual predation at the expense of not covering many other important topics. Most presentations featured real-life examples of youth stalked through a MySpace or Facebook account. Information was often conveyed in a way that turned kids off rather than turning them on to responsible computing.[12]

The authors recall one school presentation made by a former police officer that showed how easy it was to cyberstalk. He pre-tended to be a stalker by targeting a particular girl who attended the local high school. In the process he mined the girl's profile for personal data, checked other Web sources to gather additional information about the girl and her friends, and then used Google Maps satellite imaging to locate and show her house and school. In effect the girl was shown to be extremely vulnerable to attacks and naive for posting personal information online. However, neither the girl nor her parents were in the audience, nor were they consulted before this "public information" was used in a community presenta-tion given to an entire school district. When the girl and her parents found out what had happened, they were mortified and complained to the school district, which was also upset that a well-meaning non-profit initiative had not vetted the presentation beforehand.

delivered online to provide instruction in how to teach and monitor students for improved cybersafety, security, and ethics. The training featured instruction specifically about cyberbullying and represented a beginning effort to design and deliver professional development needed by school personnel throughout the United States.

Unfortunately, too many school administrators and teachers still find themselves without training or resources, and also at a legal disadvantage to deal with online bullying and stalking in which students are involved. Unless bullying or stalking messages show evidence of being criminal in nature, or are accessed by students from school grounds, or in some way disrupt a school's overall educational process—precedents set by previous court cases—students have the right to free speech just as every other citizen does. As such, some cyberstalking and cyberbullying cases that take place off campus, but between students at the same school, fall outside the jurisdiction of school officials. In such cases school districts can find themselves in very difficult positions, caught between parents who demand punishment for those behind the attacks and the law, which may protect bullying or stalking that takes place online yet does not rise to the level of being criminal in nature. In criminal cases school officials are obligated to notify law enforcement officials. In many ways these conditions can act as a disincentive for school administrators to attempt to handle cases of online abuse themselves in relatively informal ways, particularly when a few wrong decisions may lead to thousands of dollars in legal costs and damages.

In 2007, during routine hallway monitoring, a New York State middle school principal discovered a student using his smart phone to view pornography. After seizing the phone he escorted the student to his office and checked the phone's Web browsing history. He discovered a ton of porn on the phone, including sexually explicit photos apparently sent to and received from other students in his school during school hours. The principal called the parents of the student from whom he had taken the phone. They were upset that the principal had invaded their son's privacy and seized his property: his phone. Other parents who had been contacted had mixed reactions, but in the main were unconcerned and unsupportive of

Police departments are expanding their computer crimes units and diversifying their methods in an attempt to catch online criminals. Officers will often pretend to be teenagers in online chat rooms or social networks in an attempt to flush out predators and bullies. *(Source: AP Photo/Oscar Sosa)*

TEN TIPS AGAINST CYBERBULLYING

Preventing cyberbullying is a mutual effort among law enforcement, educators, schools, and parents. A plethora of information has been researched to gather tips for parents to use in preventing cyberbullying or to help them determine if their child is being cyberbullied. Sameer Hinduja and Justin W. Patchin from the respected Cyberbullying Research Center have compiled 10 tips for parents:[14]

1. Establish proper rules for interacting with people in society. Illustrate that cyberbullying inflicts harm.
2. Research as to what schools have Internet Safety educational programs.
3. Provide education to your children on appropriate Internet use and behaviors.
4. Be a good role-model in technology usage (i.e., do not harass others online).
5. Always monitor the child's use of the technology. Do not spy, but participate in the usage. Place the technology in a visible location.
6. Install filtering and blocking software. Use this as part of your online safety education, but not as a solo preventative.
7. Always watch for abnormal signs when your child uses their technology.
8. Use an "Internet Use Contract" or "Cell Phone Use Contract" to clearly determine what is appropriate use and communication.
9. Maintain open-ended communication with your child about issues in cyberspace.
10. Reinforce positive morals and values with others.

the principal's actions, which admittedly were not based on obvious disruption to the school learning environment nor related to cyberbullying much less cyberstalking. Police also declined to treat the matter as a violation of child pornography laws, although if this incident occurred today police would be much more inclined to investigate and seek prosecution for sexting (i.e., possessing or distributing "pseudo child pornography"). For his part, the principal felt uncertain about what should or could be done to intervene in school conduct of this sort. Many schools districts are now adopting "no or limited cell phone use" policies to prevent these kinds of potentially disruptive situations from developing.

PARENT AND ADULT ROLE MODELING AND SUPERVISION

Parent and adult role models face an important challenge in interacting with their children to keep them safe. Life with the Internet exposes children to strangers from across the world and to information that is available with a few clicks of the mouse. As a result, one of the most important steps parents and adult role models must take is to form a trusting relationship with their children.

Spying and constantly looking over a child's shoulder only makes that child find new ways to hide information. Thus building a relationship that allows children to feel comfortable talking with their parents about difficult situations or their activities is important. Furthermore, as so-called digital immigrants (people who did not grow up using IT), it is important for parents to understand the technology that their children are using.[13] Accessing the sites they use, such as Myspace or Facebook, is one way to understand how children communicate online. Learning how to communicate through texting or how to use cell phones is important. Parents and adult role models must act in the ways they want their children to act. For example, if parents are staying online for hours of gaming and posting inappropriate content online, children will follow suit. As a result, developing good cyberethics and behaviors is important in preventing online victimization.

CONCLUSION

Given the complexities of cyberstalking and cyberbullying issues, a wide range of people are needed to keep watch and protect against attacks. Currently policy makers are attempting to craft more effective laws, school administrators are struggling to work out what is within their legal bounds, law enforcement officers are developing cybercrime and Internet Crimes Against Children task forces, and parents and guardians are striving to better understand the everyday lives of young people online. Progress is being made to develop and make available sound education programs in cybersafety, security, and ethics. Reputable instructional resources such as i-SAFE and NetSmartz already exist and are widely used in schools by teachers and from homes by parents. Kids can also directly access and use these resources on their own.

Despite all of these various factors working toward maintaining the Internet as a safe and effective mode of communication, it is unlikely that online abuse will ever entirely cease to be a problem for Internet users. Furthermore, those who are actually experiencing potentially harmful attacks are often the only ones positioned to decide whether or not something that might appear to others as harmful—like joking around or overbearing romantic gestures— actually represents bullying or stalking. As such, people online every day, communicating with others, are also the best positioned to stop online abuse by choosing not to cause harm to others, and deciding to become good cybercitizens.

Avoiding and Preventing Online Abuse

When it comes to Internet safety, the online activities and concerns of young users matter a great deal. In 2009, students from Washington, D.C., participated in briefing a high-level, important committee about their online experiences and what needed to be done to make the Internet safer. Their input was carefully listened to and considered along with testimony from many adult experts representing social computing firms, Internet service providers, secondary and higher education, law enforcement, parents, and other stakeholder groups. In effect, kids were given a voice by the Online Safety and Technology Working Group commissioned by the National Technology Information Administration, which had been charged by Congress to explore and make recommendations for improving Internet safety for young people. The committee's final report, Youth Safety on a Living Internet, was issued in June 2010.[1] The information it contains is now being used in many ways by federal and state government officials; Internet, software engineering,

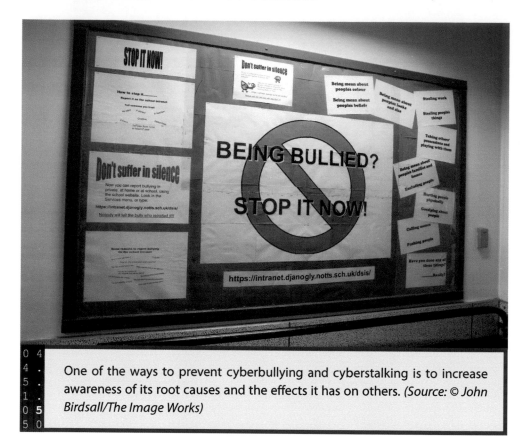

One of the ways to prevent cyberbullying and cyberstalking is to increase awareness of its root causes and the effects it has on others. *(Source: © John Birdsall/The Image Works)*

and social computing firms; and educators throughout America, to develop and implement changes to meet the needs of young users everywhere.

EDUCATION—LEARNING ABOUT REALITIES AND MYTHS

According to researchers, several myths exist about cyberstalking and cyberbullying. Youth, parents, school officials, and community members must understand the facts of cyberbullying and stalking to protect against future incidents and teach proper cyberethics. In fact many of these myths are what allow bullying or stalking behavior online to continue, without the notice of authorities. So knowing about the myths of cyberbullying can itself be used as a significant way to prevent it. In their work on cyberbullying, McQuade, Colt, and Meyer provide a description of these myths.[2]

1. Bullying Helps Victims Toughen Up

Many people believe that bullying and stalking behavior, online or off-line, is good for people because it helps them to become stronger in a harsh world. This is clearly not the case, as has been demonstrated repeatedly by those victims who have become depressed, hurt others after being bullied, or hurt themselves as a result of bullying or stalking. Even if it were true that bullying helped victims "toughen up," the myth still ignores the physical and financial damages that often accompany bullying, including permanent disability, hospital or therapy bills, and legal costs.

2. Bullying Is a "Normal" Part of Childhood Development

Bullying is such a widespread phenomenon, particularly among youth, that it can seem as if it is just something that people "naturally" do as part of their "normal" life. Think about what those words imply. Effectively, when people say that something like bullying is "normal" or "natural," what they are saying is that nothing can, or should, be done about it, regardless of how bad it is. As a society, we decide what "normal" and "natural" is, which is precisely why we make laws against the kinds of behaviors that make up bullying and stalking.

3. Bullying and Stalking Is Sometimes Just Playing or Goofing Around

It can often be difficult to decide on what bullying is because people may have different perspectives on what happened in any given incident. A "bully" might think he was just playing, while a "victim" might feel genuinely hurt. Similarly, a "stalker" might think she is being romantic, while a "victim" might be afraid to go home out of fear that the stalker is inside. However, even when people do not mean to hurt other people, the fact remains that someone has been harmed. As such, bullying and stalking cannot be ignored simply because "bullies" and "stalkers" might have good intentions.

4. When Bullying or Stalking Becomes Serious, Someone Will Tell the Authorities

While people often notify the authorities when bullying or stalking issues become particularly harmful, that certainly is not always the case. Bullies and stalkers frequently use threats as a way to prevent victims from contacting the authorities. Thus victims often believe that going for help will simply result in more frequent or more harmful abuse. In cyberstalking and cyberbullying cases, youth often fear that merely telling an adult about their problems will result in being banned from using computers or the Internet as a way to protect them from further abuse.

Many children who are victimized by bullies and stalkers often respond when asked about reporting the incidents with statements such as, "I would never tell anyone—it would make things worse." Research has shown that students and bystanders are reluctant to inform others about the incident because they feel like they will not be properly acknowledged. Furthermore, those in leadership positions such as school administrators will not do anything if presented with such information. Finally, the idea that "someone else" will handle bullying or stalking problems simply makes it that much easier for perpetrators to go unnoticed—when everyone thinks that a problem is "someone else's," then nobody ends up getting involved to stop the problem.

5. Parents or Employers of Offenders Know About Stalking or Bullying, and Will Put a Stop to It

This statement is a myth for a variety of reasons related to other myths. First, stalking and bullying behaviors can often go unnoticed by parents or employers, particularly when victims or bystanders fail to report incidents of abuse. Even when incidents of abuse are reported, parents or employers who believe some of the other myths—such as myths one, two, or three—simply choose to ignore it. Just as with Myth 4, this myth can act as yet another excuse for people to avoid taking action to prevent further abuse.

6. Most Bullying and Stalking Takes Place on School Grounds or At Places of Employment

While this myth may once have been true, it certainly is no longer the case. Information technologies allow bullying and stalking to take place wherever a victim can be contacted. With mobile devices as prevalent as they are, bullying and stalking can take place anywhere, and at any time. This myth can be dangerous simply because some people may not realize how easily accessible victims of bullying and stalking really are, believing that homes provide safe grounds.

7. Physical Bullying Is More Common than Verbal Bullying

This is another myth that can be used to label ongoing forms of abuse as non-harmful. Forms of verbal bullying are much more common than physical bullying, according to McQuade, Colt, and Meyers. As such, incidents that look as if they might be bullying, even though they do not involve physical violence, often warrant further investigation.

Nearly all of these myths seem to just "make sense" at a simple level—but that does not make them true. In a way, they act as "stories" that are passed around from person to person, and the more people that believe the stories, the easier bullying and stalking becomes for offenders. By fighting the myths of cyberstalking and cyberbullying, more people can better understand and more effectively prevent forms of online abuse. Just knowing how forms of abuse work, however, will not always completely protect against them from happening. In order to do that, people need to change behaviors and take action.

CHOOSE TO BE A GOOD CYBERCITIZEN AND NOT CAUSE HARM ONLINE

Avoiding and preventing cyberstalking and cyberbullying, along with a number of other forms of abuse, really comes down to one

HOW CAN I PREVENT CYBERBULLYING?

The National Crime Prevention Council (NCPC) is a nonprofit organization that for many years has devoted itself to helping people understand what they can do to prevent crime. This is the organization that sponsors McGruff the Crime Dog programs and slogans such as, "Take a bite out of crime." On its Web site the NCPC features the following tips from teens on how to prevent cyberbullying:[3]

- Refuse to pass along cyberbullying messages
- Tell friends to stop cyberbullying
- Block communication with cyberbullies
- Report cyberbullying to a trusted adult

You can also help prevent cyberbullying by:

- Speaking with other students, as well as teachers and school administrators, to develop rules against cyberbullying
- Raising awareness of the cyberbullying problem in your community by holding an assembly and creating fliers to give to younger kids or parents
- Sharing NCPC's anti-cyberbullying message with friends

Don't forget that even though you can't see a cyberbully or the bully's victim, cyberbullying causes real problems. If you wouldn't say it in person, don't say it online. Delete cyberbullying. Don't write it. Don't forward it.

thing: becoming a good cybercitizen. Respect for others, an ability to stay calm, a willingness to help others, and the knowledge of how to appropriately use various forms of information technologies is all part of that goal. It is about making the spaces where Internet users and their friends come together online more of a community and less of a potential threat. All of that begins, of course, with respect.

Learn About Respect

Teaching community values to children is an important aspect of preventing cyberstalking and cyberbullying. Understanding that children must respect their peers and elders can further promote positive relationships. It is also important that children understand the consequences of their actions and the consequences if one tries to victimize peers. Taking the stance that disrespect while online or off-line will not be tolerated by community members can also help kids. By taking a proactive approach among children, parents, teachers, law enforcement, and community members, a message of respect can be sent.

For many children, the process of learning respect begins at a very young age. "Please" and "Thank you," for many, are just the beginning stages. By offering thanks, someone can build respect and trust among friends, teachers, and parents. As children grow older, respect is an integral part of school, and teachers further promote such behavior. In some cases teachers use stickers, awards, and extra recess as ways to instill the importance of respect among each other.

Other avenues also exist for children to learn about respect. By participating in sports, musical programs, scouting groups, or other extracurricular activities, youth can learn how to positively interact with their peers. It may seem like a simple thing, but cultivating a respect for others goes a long way toward preventing bullying, stalking, and other forms of harm and abuse. It is a simple concept: Treat other people as you would wish to be treated yourself. Those who follow such a concept would be much less likely to become bullies or stalkers themselves, as it is somewhat improbable that anyone really wants to be bullied or stalked in any way that would seriously harm or scare them. Having this form of respect for others can often be difficult, because it is not always possible to see what things are like from someone else's perspective. Often this is the way bullying or stalking can accidentally take place—but this should not prevent people from at least attempting to be respectful of the positions of others.

Keep It Together and Ignore Attackers

It is common for people to have a bad day. Missing the school bus, not doing well on an exam, or not being selected for a sports team can be very stressful and make anyone feel bad. Anyone can make mistakes or not have the best day, so it is important for people to make sure they do not take their bad feelings out on others. These small changes in mood brought about by stress or anger can often be the tiny push needed to drive someone toward a malicious act. However, putting someone down by bullying or stalking is never the answer. In fact, bullying or stalking someone not only hurts the victim of the abusive behavior, but also often results in severe punishments for the person responsible, which can be a considerable amount of trouble simply because someone had a stressful day.

It is important to talk about problems with stress or anger with someone who can be trusted. By doing so, anyone can make the smart decision in harnessing stressful feelings and recovering from a bad day. Keeping it together can be important not only for those who may become stressed and lash out at others, but additionally for those who are victims of bullies or stalkers themselves.

One of the best ways to prevent further abuse after an initial attack has been made is to simply ignore the attacker and get away from them. This is often harder than it sounds, however, particularly when a verbal attack is meant to provoke a response. Not responding, however, can often successfully show a bully or stalker that their attacks are not successful and lead to them not contacting victims anymore. Determined abusers, especially stalkers not motivated by eliciting a response from a victim, will not be dissuaded by simply ignoring their communications. Most Web sites and services that allow people to communicate with one another, including online games, instant messaging, and social networking sites, allow users to block one another. Blocking a user and preventing further attacks is often as simple as the click of a button. So, in an online attack, simply stay cool, block the attacker, go do something else, and tell someone about the incident.

Stand Up For Victims

Anyone who has ever been bullied by their peers knows how important it is to have someone there to talk to. Being harassed,

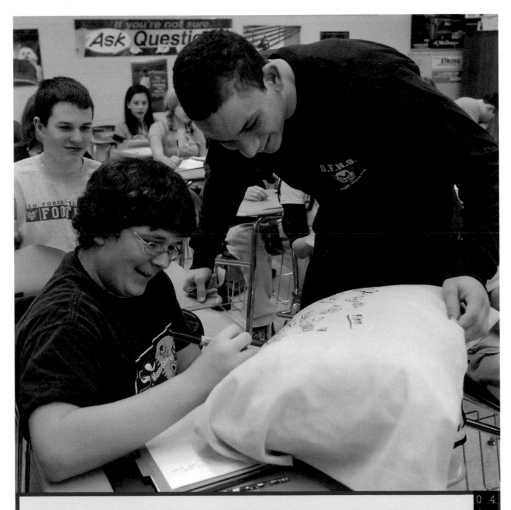

In 2008, more than 220 schools participated in International Stand Up to Bully Day. Students encouraged others to support bullying victims and to sign an anti-bullying pledge. *(Source: AP Photo/The Times-Tribune, Jason Farmer)*

intimidated, or picked on can make a person feel useless, and the worst thing that can happen is for her to not have anyone to talk to. Guidance counselors, peers, or parents can be very helpful in assisting victims when they have been bullied. Simply providing an outlet for a victim to talk about what happened can be quite calming and assuring to the victim.

It is important for victims to feel comfortable talking about the attack. Furthermore, it is also important for victim advocates to act publicly in support of a victim's rights and the prevention of cyberbullying and stalking. Without feeling comfortable and knowing that people are available and willing to help, victims will feel alone and uneasy about seeking help. As a result, parents, teachers, guidance counselors, and peers should speak openly about the fact that bullying will not be tolerated in their community. Similarly, should anyone find themselves witness to any form of online attack or stalking, their silence can only make things easier on the attacker to continue the abusive behavior.

Becoming an online vigilante is not a good response, however, as many online bullies or attackers simply want to get a reaction out of someone. As such, "protectors" can quickly find themselves in the position of the victim. While getting in the middle of such an attack can often make matters worse for everyone involved, bystanders can notify authorities about the problem, and provide support for the victim. Online anonymity can work against the harm done by attackers, in the sense that friends can easily, and without the bully's knowledge, send messages of support even in the middle of an attack. Sometimes a quick, friendly message is all it takes to take the sting out of a bullying attempt.

Be Wary of "Online Strangers"

Growing up, children have always been taught the idea of "stranger danger" and to stay away from strangers. For teens growing up, requesting to go out in public with their friends often comes with a conversation about making sure not to talk with strangers and to make sure they stick together with their friends. With the advent of social computing, however, young people do not need to leave the comforts of their homes to meet up with strangers or get into dangerous situations. Young people have increased access to strangers from all areas of the world through the use of social computing and IT devices. One can experience cyberbullying or stalking just by updating a Facebook status or chatting on a gaming forum. Even after being told about the dangers of strangers, it is common for young people to engage in communication with new people they meet online. Social networking sites and gaming forums allow them to meet various people from different locations and backgrounds. Meeting new people one would normally never contact in the absence of the Internet can certainly be a good thing, but it can be next to impossible to verify that anyone is really who they say they are online. Deceiving someone by crafting a convincing identity is often the best way to begin many different kinds of online abuse, including bullying, stalking, and predation. While these things are not that common, the possibility that someone online might not be who they say they are should never be completely ignored. As such, always remember that online, a little bit of paranoia can go a long way toward protection against online abuse, particularly when things begin to get uncomfortably personal.

Be Honest—But Not Too Honest

It is a common practice to lie about age, gender, and location online. Young people do this for numerous reasons, including trying to protect their identity from strangers or to engage in activities they might be prohibited from based on their age. Adults and other computer users can also lie about their age, gender, and location. It is important for youth to identify who they are truly conversing with and for what purposes. Depending on the topic of conversation, adults may find themselves in legal trouble when talking with minors. That said, the topics of conversation that an adult could get in trouble over might be a little too personal for discussion with online strangers. Playing with online identity and using information

to one's advantage online is usually okay, unless it is used to deliberately deceive other people in a malicious way. Filling out profile
information with vague references and jokes is one thing; pretending to be someone else online to embarrass someone is something
very different. Here, being a little bit paranoid comes into play as
well—being honest online is about not harming people with the
way one presents oneself, while also making sure to avoid disclosing
too much personal information. On the one hand, too little good
information might be seen as deceptive or malicious; on the other,
too much information could be used by bullies or stalkers to start
an attack. The trick is in finding a good balance between the two.

Responsible Use of the Internet and IT Devices—
It Is Up to Everyone

As computing technologies become part of people's everyday lives,
it is important that children and adults take responsibility for their
computing behaviors and learn how to properly protect themselves
online. When purchasing a new device, it is important for both parents and children to understand the dangers of the technology as
well as the expected positive benefits. Furthermore, safe computing
includes understanding how to properly maintain one's computer
and use security software to protect against malicious attacks. If a
person is unaware of how to manage his computer's security settings,
training is another step one can take to help maintain and learn
about computing technology. Overall, common sense as it relates to
responsible computing is crucial. The Internet never forgets and, as
a result, one must consider the consequences of posting information,
including pictures, before doing so.

Report Cyberstalking and Cyberbullying

Finally, it is important that both victims and bystanders report incidents of both online and off-line abuse. Often, in the absence of any
form of enforcement or punishment, bullying and stalking behaviors
can go on for months or years. The effects of such long-term abuse
can be devastating to individual victims, bullies, families, schools,

USE ONGUARD ONLINE

Among the very best online resources for understanding and dealing with cyberstalking and cyberbullying is OnGuard Online (http://www.onguardonline.gov/). This Web site is hosted by the Federal Trade Commission in partnership with numerous other federal government entities and the Internet Education Foundation. The site provides useful information about how to avoid Internet scams, remain safe and secure online, responsibly enjoy social computing, and dispose of old computers to protect confidential information and the environment, among many other special topics. Just about everything people should know and practice when using the Internet can be found at OnGuard Online. And it is fortunate that the Web site features games and videos that young people can enjoy and learn from.[4]

and communities. In developing plans within school, community, and work environments, it is important to detail where victims can report incidents and obtain assistance. Schools can designate certain school officials and teachers to handle incidents of cyberstalking and cyberbullying. These officials can be trained to handle such situations and can train other teachers to handle bullying cases within their classrooms. In a community setting it is important for local law enforcement to care about such cases, if reported by victims, that are similar to any other crime reported. Lastly, workplace settings should be similar to that of schools by having representatives to handle such cases in an appropriate manner that positively assists the victim.

CONCLUSION

Trying to be a good cybercitizen goes a long way toward preventing abuse online—both as an attacker and as a victim. Unfortunately, it can often be a difficult task. People say mean things intended to provoke anger and stress among complete strangers every day, and it can be so easy to join in, particularly with so many other people participating. Regardless, remember that the waves of attacks faced by victims online are comprised of the small, yet hurtful, actions of hundreds of other Internet users. If everyone would strive just a little harder to become more respectful cybercitizens, many of the immensely upsetting attacks that cause so much damage could ultimately be prevented.

CHRONOLOGY

1971 First e-mail application is created by Ray Tomlinson while employed at ARPA, becoming basis of ARPA network called ARPANET, the forerunner of Internet.

1975 Microsoft Corporation is founded by William "Bill" Henry Gates III and Paul Allen.

1976 Apple Computers is founded by Steven Jobs and Ron Wayne.

First unsolicited e-mail advertisement was sent from one employee—Gary Thuerk—of DEC (Digital Equipment Corporation, inventor of the minicomputer) to 400 other users of ARPANET.

1979 Cellular phones are introduced in Sweden by the Ericsson Company.

Emergence of hacker subculture.

1982 William Gibson coins the term *cyberspace* in the July 1982 edition of *Omni* magazine with his story "Burning Chrome."

1983 More than 100 companies make personal computers. Five million desktop computers are estimated to exist in the United States alone. Approximately 3 million computer terminals are now "networked" with larger "host" computers.

1984 Internet begins operations.

1990 Multimedia PCs are developed, schools begin to use videodiscs, and object-oriented multimedia authoring tools are in wide use. Simulations and educational databases are also being delivered on CD-ROM discs, many with animation.

1993 With commercialization, the Internet becomes known as the World Wide Web, and Microsoft releases Windows NT and Mosaic Web Browser.

FBI first uses Internet in criminal investigation to identify and capture "Unabomber" Ted Kaczynski.

Michigan becomes the first state to pass a stalking law that included the words *electronic harassment.*

1995   *Kim v. Bellevue School District–Newport High School* involves a senior honor student who created a Web site that discussed his friends and their obsessions with sex and football.

1996   Congress passes the Interstate Stalking Act, United States Code Title 18, 2261A, making it a crime for any person to travel across state lines with intent to injure or harass another person

Congress passes federal legislation, 47 United States Code 230 Communications Decency Act (CDA).

1997   The term *weblog* is coined by Jorn Barger.

1998   In the case of *O'Brien v. Westlake City School Board of Education,* an Ohio student receives a 10-day suspension for creating a Web site while off-campus that included pictures and insults against the school's band teacher.

2000   Interstate Stalking Act amends as part of the Violence Against Women Act (VAWA), which extends the federal stalking statute to stalking that occurs by mail, telephone, or Internet.

Beidler v. North Thurston School District No. 3 involved a student who created a Web site while at home that had doctored photos of the assistant principal doing such things as drinking alcohol and making graffiti.

I LOVE YOU (Love Bug) worm is released, striking computers all over the world.

With the "Love Bug" virus providing a reminder of the problem of cybercrime and other kinds of mischief on the Internet, leaders from the Group of Eight countries meet to see what can be done. The 41-nation Council of Europe works with the United States, Canada, Japan, and South America to draft a treaty to standardize laws against Internet crime.

Cyberstalkers Act of 2000, a bill to amend Title 18, is sponsored by Senator Abraham Spencer of Michigan. On July 27, 2000, the bill is referred to Senate committee.

Dante Michael Soiu is convicted of stalking after sending numerous packages, e-mails, and letters to Gwyneth Paltrow's residence.

2001 Following September 11 ("9-11") terrorist attacks involving U.S. jet airliners, Congress passes the U.S. Patriot Act. America's "war on terrorism" extends to international crime and cyberterrorism, with prison sentences for hacking and other forms of computer-enabled crimes dramatically increased.

Wikipedia launches and shortly becomes one of the most visited sites on the Web and demonstrates possibilities of harnessing the "Wisdom of Crowds," a fundamental aspect of what becomes known as "Web 2.0."

2003 MySpace is created.

2004 Facebook is founded by Mark Zuckerberg, a student of Harvard University. The new social computing Web site is initially limited to other college students attending Harvard. By 2006, anyone older than 13 years of age can join.

2005 YouTube is created by three former PayPal employees. The San Bruno-based service uses Adobe Flash technology to host and display user-generated video content, including video-blogging and short original videos.

2006 Megan Meier commits suicide as a result of a cruel cyberhoax and is known as the first death as a result of cyberbullying.

2007 Professor Sam McQuade and associates of the Rochester Institute of Technology conduct world's largest computer crime and victimization report revealing that a majority of 40,000 kindergarten–12th grade students surveyed experience various forms of online abuse including cyberbullying, which for many begins in kindergarten.

Wisniewski v. Board of Education of Weedsport CSD involves an eighth grader who was suspended after creating a drawing that suggested a teacher be shot and killed and sharing the drawing with other students via instant message from a home computer.

Jack Jordan is arrested for attempted coercion, aggravated harassment, and stalking of Uma Thurman.

Thirty-two Australian teenagers are prosecuted for sexting (i.e., sending nude photos of themselves in instant computer or cell phone text messages).

2010 Phoebe Prince of South Hadley, Massachusetts, commits suicide on January 14, after repeated harassment from numerous classmates.

More than 2 billion people are estimated to use computers connected to the Internet.

● ● ● ENDNOTES ● ● ●

INTRODUCTION

1. Associated Press, "States Pushing for Laws to Curb Cyberbullying," FOX News, http://www.foxnews.com/story/0,2933,253259,00.html (Accessed February 21, 2007).

2. James P. Colt, "Cyber Bullying, Threats, Harassment and Stalking," in *The Encyclopedia of Cybercrime,* Samuel C. McQuade (ed) (Westport, Conn.: Greenwood Press, 2009) 41–43.

CHAPTER 1

1. John Suler, "The Online Disinhibition Effect," *Cyber Psychology and Behavior,* 7 (August 2004): 321–26.

2. Samuel C. McQuade, James P. Colt, and Nancy B.B. Meyer, *Cyber Bullying: Protecting Kids and Adults from Online Bullies* (Westport, Conn.: Praeger, 2009) 29–36.

3. Ibid., 31.

CHAPTER 2

1. David Kushner, "Linkin Park's Mysterious Cyberstalker." *Wired Magazine,* http://www.wired.com/entertainment/music/news/2007/05/ff_linkinpark?currentPage=1 (Accessed November 17, 2010).

2. Keith Sullivan, *The Anti-bullying Handbook* (New York: Oxford University Press, 2000).

3. McQuade, Colt, and Meyer, 2009, 29.

4. Samuel C. McQuade and Neel Sampat, *RIT Survey of Internet and At-risk Behaviors* (Rochester, N.Y.: Rochester Institute of Technology, 2008).

5. Dan Olweus, *Bullying at School* (Cornwall, UK: MPG Books, 1993).

6. McQuade and Sampat, 2008.

7. Janis Wolak, Kimberley J. Mitchell, and David Finkelhor, "Online Victimization of Youth: Five Years Later," Washington, D.C.: National Center for Missing and Exploited Children, 2006.

8. Katrina Baum, Shannan Catalano, Michael Rand, and Kristina Rose, *Stalking Victimization in the United States,* Washington, D.C.: U.S. Department of Justice, Bureau of Justice Statistics, 2009.

9. Michele L. Ybarra, et al., "Internet Prevention Messages: Targeting the Right Online Behaviors," *Archives of Pediatrics and Adolescent Medicine,* 161, no. 2 (February 2007): 138–145.

10. McQuade and Sampat, 2009.

11. Ibid.

12. Ibid.

13. Baum, et. al, 2009.

CHAPTER 3

1. Emily Bazelon, "What Really Happened to Phoebe Prince? The Untold Story of Her Suicide and the Role of the Kids Who Have Been Criminally Charged for It," *Slate.com,* http://www.slate.com/id/2260952/entry/2260953/ (Accessed August 17, 2011).

2. Russell Goldman, "Teens Indicted After Allegedly Taunting Girl Who Hanged Herself," *ABC News*, http://abcnews.go.com/Technology/TheLaw/teens-charged-bullying-mass-girl-kill/story?id=10231357 (Accessed August 17, 2011).

3. Ibid.

4. NetSmartz, "Cyberbullying: Broken Friendship (video)," National Center for Missing and Exploited Children, http://www.netsmartz.org/stories/friendship.htm (Accessed August 17, 2011).

5. Sampat, Neel, "Leetspeak," in *The Encyclopedia of Cybercrime*, Samuel C. McQuade (ed) (Westport, Connecticut: Greenwood Press, 2009).

6. Ibid.

7. Ibid.

8. Ibid.

CHAPTER 4

1. Aeusenbe, "Bully Incident #18—Cyberbullying Origin: The Telephone," Bullying Stories, http://bullyinglte.wordpress.com/2009/11/10/cyberbullying-origin-the-telephone/ (Accessed June 21, 2011).

2. Associated Press, "Girl, 12, Charged With Distributing Nude Pic of Classmate," Fox News, http://www.foxnews.com/story/0,2933,370987,00.html (Posted June 25, 2008).

3. Moreno, Ivan, "Kids Won't Face Charges for Nude Pix," *Rocky Mountain News*, http://blogs.rockymountainnews.com/rockytalklive/archives/2007/03/no_charges_for_nude_teen_

phone.html (Accessed August 8, 2011).

4. Android Market home page, https://market.android.com/details?id=com.spyparent.bullyblock (Accessed June 21, 2011).

5. Suzanne Struglinski, "Schoolyard Bullying Has Gone High-Tech: Shurtleff Part of Effort to Protect Youths from Cyber-Harassment," *Deseret News*, http://www.deseretnews.com/article/645194065/Schoolyard-bullying-has-gone-high-tech.html (Accessed June 22, 2011).

6. Caroline McCarthy, "MySpace Agrees to Social-Networking Safety Plan," The Social, CNET News, http://news.cnet.com/8301-13577_3-9849909-36.html (Accessed June 22, 2010).

7. Ki Mae Huessner, "Apple Responds to iPhone Tracking Controversy," ABC News, http://abcnews.go.com/Technology/apple-responds-iphone-tracking-controversy/story?id=13468295 (Accessed June 22, 2011).

8. Daily Tech, "Apple is Tracking iPhone, iPad Users' Location; Easily Mapped With OS X App," http://www.dailytech.com/Apple+is+Tracking+iPhone+iPad+Users+Location+Easily+Mapped+With+OS+X+App/article21429.htm (Accessed August 8, 2011).

CHAPTER 5

1. Wolak, Janis, Kimberley J. Mitchell, and David Finkelhor, *Online Victimization of Youth: Five Years Later*, (Alexandria, Va.: NCMEC, 2006) 40.

2. Baum, et. al., 2009.

3. Turley, Johathan,"Bullying's Day in Court; From Hall Monitors to Personal Injury Lawyers: Parents Send a Message by Forcing Bullies from the Schoolhouse to the Courthouse," *USA Today*, http://www.usatoday.com/printedition/news/20080715/opledetuesdayx.art.htm (Posted July 15, 2008).

4. Julian Margaret Gibbs, "Bullying: Justice Is Better than Vengeance," *The Independent*, http://www.independent.co.uk/news/education/education-news/bullying-justice-is-better-than-vengeance-444242.html (Posted April 12, 2007).

CHAPTER 6

1. Bill Hewitt, Siobhan Morrisey, and Pam Grout, "Did a Cruel Hoax Lead to Suicide?" *People*, 68, no. 23 (December 2007): 135–136.

2. Associated Press, "States Pushing for Laws to Curb Cyberbullying," Fox News, http://www.foxnews.com/story/0,2933,253259,00.html (Accessed June 6, 2008).

3. Ibid.

4. Kim Zetter, "Judge Acquits Lori Drew in Cyberbullying Case, Overrules Jury," Wired.com, http://www.wired.com/threatlevel/2009/07/drew_court/ (Accessed June 23, 2011).

5. Nowt News, "US Weighs Criminal Penalties for Cyber-Bullying," NowtNews.com, http://nowtnews.com/05674/us-weighs-criminal-penalties-for-cyber-bullying/ (Accessed June 23, 2011).

6. Ibid.

7. KIRO TV, "Man Charged In Prolific Cyberstalking Case; Police Search For More Victims," KIRO TV, http://www.kirotv.com/news/25404771/detail.html (Accessed June 23, 2011).

8. Levi Pulkkinen, "Cyberstalker Who Terrorized Teen Gets 5 1/2 Years," Komo News, http://www.komonews.com/news/local/117437423.html (Accessed June 23, 2011).

9. Alyssa Chin, "Police Try to Prevent Cyber Bullying," KKTV News, http://www.kktv.com/home/headlines/Police_Try_To_Prevent_Cyber_Bullying_121227869.html (Accessed June 23, 2011).

10. Sandy Harris, Garth Petrie, and William Willoughby, "Bullying at School: A Canadian Perspective," *National Association of Secondary School Principals Bulletin*, 86, no. 630 (March 2002): 3–14.

11. Teen Caravan, "Cyber Bully-Teen," *Fight Crime: Invest in Kids*, (Princeton, N.J.: Opinion Research Corporation, 2006).

12. Nathan Fisk, "Trash Talk and Trusted Adults: An Analysis of Youth Internet Safety Discourses in New York State," Unpublished Doctoral Dissertation (draft report and defense), Troy, N.Y.: Rensselaer Polytechnic Institute, 2011.

13. Marc Prensky, *Digital Natives, Digital Immigrants*, (University of Nebraska University Press, 2001) 1–6.

14. Justin W. Patchin and Sameer Hinduja. "Preventing Cyberbullying: Top Ten Tips for Parents." Cyberbulling

Research Center. http://www
.cyberbullying.us/Top_Ten_
Tips_Parents_Cyberbully-
ing_Prevention.pdf (Accessed
June 23, 2011.)

CHAPTER 7

1. Online Safety Technology
   Working Group, "Youth Safety
   on a Living Internet," Washington, D.C.: National Technology
   Information Administration,
   U.S. Department of Commerce,
   2010.

2. McQuade, Colt, and Meyer,
   2009.

3. National Crime Prevention
   Council, 2011, "How Can I
   Prevent Cyberbullying?" http://
   www.ncpc.org/newsroom/
   current-campaigns/cyberbully
   ing (Accessed June 24,
   2011).

4. Federal Trade Commission,
   "OnGuard Online," http://www
   .onguardonline.gov/ (Accessed
   June 24, 2011).

# BIBLIOGRAPHY

Anderson, Nate. "Cyberbullying and Schools: Where does a Principal's Authority End?" *Arstechnica.com*. Available online. URL: http://arstechnica.com/news.ars/post/20070222-8903.html Accessed February 23, 2007.

Associated Press. "Girl, 12, Charged With Distributing Nude Pic of Classmate." *Fox News*. Available online. URL: http://www.foxnews .com/story/0,2933,370987,00.html Accessed June 25, 2008.

Bartlett, Lawrence. "Bullies In Cyberspace Spark Growing Concern." *Spacewar.com*. Available online. URL: http://www.spacewar .com/reports/Bullies_In_Cyberspace_Spark_Growing_Concern_ 999.html Accessed July 16, 2007.

Burgess-Proctor, Amanda, Justin W. Patchin, and Sameer Hinduja. "Cyberbullying and Online Harassment: Reconceptualizing the Victimization of Adolescent Girls." In *Female Victims of Crime: Reality Reconsidered*, Vanessa Garcia and Janice Clifford (eds.) Upper Saddle River, N.J.: Prentice Hall, 2008.

Cassel, David. "Schoolboards: Net Dangers Over-Rated; Bring Social Networks to School." *Tech.blorge.com*. Available online. URL: http://tech.blorge.com/Structure:%20/2007/08/07/school-boards-net-dangers-over-rated-bring-social-networks-to-school/ Accessed August 27, 2007.

Carpenter, Deborah, and Christopher J. Ferguson. *The Everything Parent's Guide to Dealing with Bullies: From Playground Teasing to Cyber Bullying, All You Need to Ensure Your Child's Safety and Happiness*. Avon, Mass.: F+W Media, Inc., 2009.

Colt, James P. "Cyber Bullying, Threats, Harassment and Stalking." In Samuel C. McQuade (ed.). *The Encyclopedia of Cybercrime*, 41–43: Greenwood Press: Westport, Conn., 2009.

Cyberbullying.US. "Research Explanation of Cyberbullying." Available online. URL: http://www.cyberbullying.us/research.php Accessed September 25, 2007.

Dunnewind, Stephanie. "Schools Trying to Prevent Harassment in Cyberspace." *The Seattle Times*. Available online. URL: http://seattletimes.nwsource.com/html/living/2003292713_school space07.html Accessed October 31, 2006.

Gallagher, Erin. "Sextortion: Online Predators are Using Technology and Peer Pressure to Blackmail our Kids." *Channahon-Minooka Patch*. Available online. URL: http://channahon-minooka.patch.com/articles/sextortion-mom-talk Accessed July 11, 2011.

Giannetti, Charlene, and Margaret Sagarese. "The Newest Breed of Bully, the Cyberbully." National Parent Teacher Association. Available online. URL: http://www.32ndpta.org/PDFs/Parents/1-Cyberbully.pdf Accessed October 11, 2006.

Hinduja, Sameer, and Justice W. Patchin. *Bullying Beyond the Schoolyard: Preventing and Responding to Cyberbullying*. Thousand Oaks, Calif.: Corwin Press, 2009.

Jacobs, Thomas A. *Teen Cyberbullying Investigated: Where Do Your Rights End and Consequences Begin?* Minneapolis, Minn.: Free Spirit Publishing Inc., 2010.

Klass, Perri. "18 and Under: At Last, Facing Down Bullies (and Their Enablers)," *New York Times*. Available online. URL: http://www.nytimes.com/2009/06/09/health/09klas.html?emc=eta1 Accessed August 17, 2011.

Kowalski, Robin M., Susan P. Limber, and Patricia W. Agatston. *Cyber Bullying: Bullying in the Digital Age*. Oxford, U.K.: Blackwell Publishing, 2008.

Li, Qing. "New Bottle But Old Wine: A Research of Cyberbullying in Schools." *Computers and Human Behavior* 23, no. 4 (2005): 2–15.

McQuade, Samuel C., James P. Colt, and Nancy B.B. Meyer. *Cyber Bullying: Protecting Kids and Adults From Online Bullies*. Westport, Conn.: Praeger, 2009.

Myers, Jill J., Donna S. McCaw, and Leaunda S. Hemphill. *Responding to Cyber Bullying: An Action Tool for School Leaders*. Thousand Oaks, Calif.: Corwin, 2011.

Pew Foundation. "Internet and American Life Survey Reports." Philadelphia, Pa., 2007.

Prensky, Marc. *Digital Natives, Digital Immigrants*. Lincoln, Neb.: University of Nebraska Press, 2001.

Princeton Survey Research Associates International. "Cyberbullying and Online Teens." Pew Foundation. Available online. URL: http://www.pewinternet.org/pdfs/PIP%20Cyberbullying%20Memo.pdf Accessed July 2, 2007.

Salazar, Cristian. "Alexis Pilkington Facebook Horror: Cyber Bullies Harass Teen Even After Suicide." Associated Press. Available online. URL: http://www.huffingtonpost.com/2010/03/24/alexis-pilkington-faceboo_n_512482.html. Accessed August 17, 2011.

Shariff, Shaheen. *Confronting Cyuber-Bullying: What Schools Need to Know to Control Misconduct and Avoid Legal Consequences*. Cambridge, U.K.: Cambridge University Press, 2009.

Shariff, Shaheen, Cyber-*Bullying: Issues and Solutions for the School, the Classroom and the Home* (New York: Routledge, 2008).

Trolley, Barbara C. and Constance Hanel, *Cyber Kids, Cyber Bullying, Cyber Balance*. Thousand Oaks, Calif.: Corwin, 2010.

Willard, Nancy E. *Cyberbullying and Cyberthreats: Responding to the Challenge of Online Social Aggression, Threats, and Distress*. Champaign, IL: Research Press, 2007.

●●● FURTHER RESOURCES ●●●

BOOKS

Bolton, Jose. *No Room for Bullies: From the Classroom to Cyberspace, Teaching Respect, Stopping Abuse and Rewarding Kindness.* Boys Town, Neb.: Boys Town Press, 2005.

Hinduja, Sameer and Justin W. Patchin. *Bullying Beyond the Schoolyard: Preventing and Responding to Cyber Bullying.* Thousand Oaks, Calif.: Sage Publications, 2009.

McQuade, III, Samuel C., James P. Colt, and Nancy B.B. Meyer. *Cyber Bullying: Preventing Online Abuse and Bullying by Kids and Adults.* Westport, Conn.: Greenwood-Praeger, 2009.

Willard, Nancy. *Cyber-Safe Kids, Cyber-Savvy Teens: Helping Young People Learn to Use the Internet Safely and Responsibly.* Hoboken, N.J.: Jossey-Bass, 2007.

DOCUMENTARIES AND DVDS

Cyberbullies. Monmouth Junction, N.J.: Meridian Education Corporation, 2006.

Uses dramatizations to spread awareness of cyberbullying.

Cyberbullying Prevention Public Service Announcements. National Crime Prevention Council, 2007.

Short audio and video segments that promote cyberethics.

Let's Fight It Together. Childnet; Department for Children, Schools and Families, 2007.

Produced in the United Kingdom, discusses pain and sadness associated with cyber victimization.

PRIMETIME: Cyberbullying—Cruel intentions. Howell, Mich.: ABC News, 2006.

Diane Sawyer discusses how computing technology amplifies discouraging youth behavior.

Stop Bullying...Take A Stand! New York: Castle Works, Inc., 2005.
    Hosted by Miss America 2003, discusses ways to prevent bullying.

WEB SITES

Bullying Stories: Dealing with Bullies from an Adult Perspective
    http://bullyinglte.wordpress.com/
    Web blog that contains stories and various kinds of resources.

Center for Democracy and Technology
    http://www.cdt.org
    Works to keep the Internet open, innovative, and free.

The Center for Information Security Awareness
    http://www.cfisa.org
    Aims to increase security awareness among various community members.

The Children's Internet Protection Act (CIPA)
    http://www.fcc.gov/guides/childrens-internete-protection-act
    Federal law that addresses offensive content viewable on school and library computers.

Cyberbully 411
    http://cyberbully411.org
    Offers educational materials for youth on cyberbullying.

Cyberbullying Research Center
    http://www.cyberbullying.us/resources.php
    Identifies the causes and consequences of online victimization.

The Cyber Safety and Ethics Initiative
http://www.rrcsei.org
Ensures cybersafety among parents, educators, and youth.

Electronic Privacy Information Center
http://epic.org
Keeps community members informed about privacy and civil liberties issues.

The Family Online Safety Institute
http://www.fosi.org
Promotes best practices in the area of online safety with respect to free expression.

Federal Bureau of Investigation Kids Page
http://www.fbi.gov/fungames/kids/kids
Covers investigation, safety, and other topics geared to kids.

Federal Communications Commission (FCC)
http://www.fcc.gov
Regulates interstate and international communications.

The Internet Keep Safe Coalition (iKeepSafe)
http://www.ikeepsafe.org
Collaboration of professionals to disseminate safety resources to families worldwide.

i-SAFE Inc.
http://www.isafe.org
Nonprofit dedicated to protecting the online activity experienced by youth.

The National Center for Missing and Exploited Children
http://www.missingkids.com
Provides information about issues related to missing and exploited children.

The National Center for Victims of Crime

http://www.ncvc.org

Assists victims with support after being victimized.

National Crime Prevention Council

http://www.ncpc.org

Provides information and resources to help prevent cyberbullying and maintain Internet safety.

National Cyber Security Alliance

http://staysafeonline.org

Supports digital citizens that utilize the Internet.

NetSmartz Workshop

http://www.netsmartz.org/Parents

Educates families and professionals about Internet concerns.

OnGuard Online

http://onguardonline.gov

Provides tips to help prevent computer crimes.

The Pew Research Center's Internet and American Life Project

http://www.pewinternet.org

"Fact tank" that provides information on online safety and education.

Stop Bullying.gov

http://www.stopbullying.gov

Disseminates information from government agencies about bullying to increase awareness, prevention, and intervention.

United States Computer Emergency Readiness Team (US-CERT)

http://www.us-cert.gov

Interacts with government entities, industry, and the community to defend against cyber attacks.

Wired Safety
  http://wiredsafety.org
  Educational resources for online safety.

Working to Halt Online Abuse
  http://haltabuse.org
  Resources for victims of online abuse.

DR. SAMUEL C. MCQUADE, III, currently serves as the Professional Studies Graduate Program director in the Center for Multidisciplinary Studies at the Rochester Institute of Technology (RIT). He holds a doctoral degree in public policy from George Mason University, and a master's degree in public administration from the University of Washington. He teaches and conducts research at RIT in areas inclusive of cybercrime, enterprise security, and career options in high-tech societies. Dr. McQuade has presented his research findings, along with its implications for Internet safety, information security, and cyberethics at major events hosted by: the American Society of Criminology, the British Society of Criminology, the U.S. Department of Homeland Security, the National Intelligence Council, the National Governors Association, the Berkman Center for Internet and Society at Harvard Law School, the Family Online Safety Institute, the Division on Addictions of Harvard Medical School, and the National Association of State Chief Information Officers. Previous books include *Understanding and Managing Cybercrime* (Pearson, 2006), *The Encyclopedia of Cybercrime* (Greenwood, 2009) and *Cyber Bullying: Protecting Kids and Adults from Online Bullies* (Praeger, 2009).

SARAH E. GENTRY is currently a graduate student in the Professional Studies Masters of Science Degree program at the Rochester Institute of Technology with course concentrations in security technology management and business. She has worked as a system administrator for both the RIT residential computing lab and the Society for the Protection and Care of Children in Rochester, New York. Sarah holds a bachelor's of applied arts and science degree in multidisciplinary studies, also from RIT.

NATHAN W. FISK is the author of *Understanding Online Piracy* (Praeger, 2009) and *Digital Piracy* (Chelsea House, 2011). He recently completed his doctoral work in the Science & Technology Studies department at Rensselaer Polytechnic Institute, having previously received a bachelor's degree in information technology, a master's degree in communications and media technologies, and a second master's degree in professional studies, all from the Rochester Institute of Technology. His dissertation research focuses on the construction and effects of youth Internet safety policies in New York State, for which he was awarded National Science Foundation grant funding. In the past, he has worked on several cybercrime and Internet safety research projects, having collaborated with organizations including the National Center for Missing and Exploited Children, Infragard, and the Recording Industry Association of America.

ABOUT THE
● ● ● CONSULTING EDITOR ● ● ●

MARCUS K. ROGERS, PH.D., is the director of the Cyber Forensics Program in the department of computer and information technology at Purdue University, a former police officer, and the editor in chief of the *Journal of Digital Forensic Practice*. He has written, edited, and reviewed numerous articles and books on cybercrime. He is a professor, university faculty scholar, and research faculty member at the Center for Education and Research in Information Assurance and Security. He is also the international chair of the Law, Compliance and Investigation Domain of the Common Body of Knowledge (CBK) committee, chair of the Ethics Committee for the Digital and Multimedia Sciences section of the American Academy of Forensic Sciences, and chair of the Certification and Test Committee – Digital Forensics Certification Board. As a police officer he worked in the area of fraud and computer crime investigations. Dr. Rogers sits on the editorial board for several professional journals. He is also a member of various national and international committees focusing on digital forensic science and digital evidence. Dr. Rogers is the author of books, book chapters, and journal publications in the field of digital forensics and applied psychological analysis. His research interests include applied cyberforensics, psychological digital crime scene analysis, cybercrime scene analysis, and cyberterrorism. He is a frequent speaker at international and national information assurance and security conferences, and guest lectures throughout the world.